D0858120

C.

Disabling Pedagogy

Disabling Pedagogy

POWER, POLITICS, AND DEAF EDUCATION

Linda Komesaroff

GALLAUDET UNIVERSITY PRESS
WASHINGTON, D.C.

Gallaudet University Press
Washington, DC 20002
http://gupress.gallaudet.edu

© 2008 by Gallaudet University
All rights reserved. Published 2008
Printed in the United States of America

Library of Congress Cataloging-in-Publication Data

Komesaroff, Linda R.
  Disabling pedagogy: power, politics, and deaf education/Linda Komesaroff.
    p. cm.
  Includes bibliographical references and index.
  ISBN-13: 978-1-56368-361-9 (hardcover: alk. paper)
  ISBN-10: 1-56368-361-X (hardcover: alk. paper)
    1. Deaf—Education—United States.   2. Deaf—United States.   3. Deaf—United
States—Social conditions.
    I. Title.
  HV2430.K65   2007
  371-91'2-dc22
                           2007020849

∞ The paper used in this publication meets the minimum requirements of American
National Standard for Information Sciences—Permanence of Paper for Printed Library
Materials, ANSI Z39.48-1984.

Contents

⌐━━⌐

Acknowledgments

M Y THANKS GO to Gallaudet University Press for the opportunity to publish my first books on deafness (see also Komesaroff 2007) and to Deakin University's Faculty of Education for providing both the intellectual space in which to pursue my passion for linguistic rights and the encouragement to do so.

Thanks also go to Marie Emmitt, who has been my academic mentor, role model, and friend; to Harlan Lane and Kristina Svartholm, whose contribution to the field of deafness first inspired me; and to the Deaf leaders whose strength and intellect I admire: Markku Jokinen, Paddy Ladd, Carol-Lee Aquiline, and others.

I also wish to acknowledge the Deaf friends, children, and acquaintances in the Deaf community who warmly welcome me into their world, educate me through their stories, and fuel my passion for justice with their ongoing struggle to be heard in a hearing world.

Finally, I am grateful to the family who raised me to value "difference."

And to John—he knows why.

Preface

THE MAJOR TOPIC of this book is the critical analysis of pedagogy in deaf education and other issues related to deafness, such as cochlear implantation. The effects of language policy and practices, as well as medical intervention, that disempower Deaf people are discussed.[1] In addition, I report on the ongoing political work in deaf education in Australian schools and courts, in which parents of deaf children have taken legal action to ensure that their children obtain access to Auslan, the native language of deaf people in Australia. Despite increasing interest in native sign language and a growing number of bilingual programs for deaf children around the world, the case studies illustrate the continuing struggle to bring about (or to resist) change in deaf education. The focus on deafness offers a poignant example for educators and other "cultural workers" that illustrates how power is located in and perpetuated by dominant groups.

Schools, in particular, are sites of social (re)production—a concept that people in the dominant culture may find difficult to grasp. The field of deaf education, in particular, can benefit from substantial critical analysis.

---

1. This text adopts the convention of capitalizing "Deaf" to distinguish the members of this cultural and linguistic group; "deaf" is used to indicate the larger group of people who may or may not be members of the Deaf community and whose language and culture are generally those of the wider society.

Traditionally it has been treated as the domain of special educators, who strive to overcome the difficulties associated with hearing loss. More recently, the sociocultural view of deafness has prompted research and academic study of Deaf culture, sign linguistics, and bilingual education. This book seeks to raise an awareness of the political nature of educational policy and practice.

Marginalized by particular power-knowledge arrangements, deaf people cope with many of the same barriers as members of other oppressed social groups. What traditionally goes on in deaf education is a striking example of educators' undertaking (or resisting) a political project aimed at restructuring the relationship between a dominant and a minority group. The struggle against structures that oppress involves not only those in the Deaf field. This work draws on broader social theories such as identity or category politics and are illustrated by numerous examples of gender, class, "race," ethnicity, and sexuality.

A sociocultural view of deafness is applied in the studies reported in this book, which takes a critical stance on current practice and develops an argument for reconstructing deaf education based on educational and social theory. Through interviews with teachers, Deaf leaders, parents, and other stakeholders in the field, the study reported in chapter 2 provides a detailed and situated account of deaf education. Chapter 3 reports a study that documented the experiences of deaf students in both teacher education and tertiary education. Chapter 4 documents a school community's shift to bilingual education, which is part of the ethnographic study of the language practices in deaf education introduced in an earlier chapter. Chapter 5 provides an analytical account of the legal cases and complaints of discrimination lodged by parents of deaf children against education providers under the Disability Discrimination Act (DDA) 1992 (Commonwealth of Australia 1992) to protest the lack of access to native sign language in the classroom.

In undertaking research in this field, I am very aware of the way in which social structures and representations of difference may be viewed through multiple "lenses," the choice of which is influenced by the viewers' knowledge and position in relation to "the other." Language and literacy are components of social relationships and are embedded in social practice. As such, there is a close relationship between language and power, and particular language forms (i.e., those valued by the dominant culture) wield more power in society: "Those who can use the language forms which the culture values are able to exert more control over their lives within that culture than those who can't" (Cambourne and Brown 1987, 261).

My approach to the field of deafness has been strongly influenced by my background as a language and literacy teacher, my understanding of and respect for the language and culture of Deaf people, and significant events and Deaf people in the Deaf World.[2] In declaring my knowledge of and interest in the language and culture of the Deaf community, I am responding to a call by a past president of the World Federation of the Deaf, Yerker Andersson (Andersson 1990). In his chapter titled "Who Should Make Decisions on Communication among Deaf People?" Andersson calls on researchers and commentators to make known their language skills and experience of Deaf culture if they choose to comment on Deaf issues, inquire into the Deaf World, or research the concerns of Deaf people.

In the late 1980s I became aware of native sign language and acquired fluency in Auslan through immersion in the Deaf community. There I was exposed to Deaf culture and grew to understand the perspective of Deaf people. I was struck by the stories I heard, in particular, Deaf people's struggle with education. Those I met drew graphic images for me of their humiliation by oral educators. Moreover, they related that they had been forced to communicate through speech and lipreading and had been denied access to Auslan throughout their school years. Deaf children from Deaf families arrived at school to find that their hearing teachers neither used nor tolerated their language. Forced to hide their hands beneath school desks, they found out-of-the-way places to use sign language in an attempt to avoid punishment. Those who were caught were forced to sit on their hands or had fingers jammed into desk drawers. The Deaf adults I met were still angry about their education.

---

2. The term "Deaf World," originally used by Deaf people in American Sign Language, indicates the linguistic minority to which they belong (see Lane, Hoffmeister, and Bahan 1996).

Because they believed their teachers' view that Auslan was the reason for their failure to become fully literate, they blamed their first language for their underachievement. And what about the system of "new signs," as they called it, being taught to their children?[3] They were dismayed.

I journeyed into the Deaf World just before the Gallaudet uprising, now recognized as a significant event in Deaf history. The protest, known as "Deaf President Now," occurred in 1988. Deaf student leaders and their allies took control of Gallaudet University to protest the appointment of the new university president. Support for the appointment of the first Deaf president had been growing, and expectations that the board would make such a selection were mounting. Six candidates were being considered for the position: three deaf and three hearing. The list was narrowed to three candidates, two of whom were deaf. But on March 6, 1988, the board (made up of predominantly hearing members) announced the appointment of Elizabeth Zinser, a hearing university administrator who had limited contact with deaf people and sign language (Malzkuhn, Covell, Hlibok, and Bourne-Firl 1994). The now-infamous comment attributed to Jane Bassett Spilman, chair of the Board of Trustees, was that "Deaf people are not ready to function in the hearing world" (Jankowski 1995, 321).

After a week in which the protesters gained national and international media attention, all of the students' demands were granted: Zinser and Spilman resigned, the board agreed to elect a majority of deaf members, no reprisals were to be taken against the protesters, and the first deaf president in the university's 124-year history, I. King Jordan, was elected (Malzkuhn et al. 1994). The protest has since been interpreted as evidence of a Deaf social movement and the response of a group marginalized by the actions of the dominant society (Jankowski 1995). In this way, cultural and political matters have always been interwoven with my understanding of deafness and native sign language.

---

3. When Deaf adults talked of the "new signs," they were referring to Australasian Signed English, a contrived sign system developed in the 1970s and generally referred to as Signed English. Younger deaf people and their parents, on the other hand, often used the term "new signs" to refer to Auslan, whose linguistic roots are found in the sign language introduced by English and Irish settlers in the early 1800s (see Branson 1993, 922; Johnston 1989, 1152).

I have also been influenced by the principles of feminist studies and other politically committed research. I draw parallels between the situation of Deaf people and the discussion of feminism by writers such as Cleo Cherryholmes (1988), Ann Oakley (Oakley 1981), and Patti Lather (1991), and I have read about politically committed research in Andrew Gitlin's (1994) edited volume on research methodology. Like Kathleen Weiler (cited in Gitlin, Siegel, and Boru 1993, 199), I, too, rejected the possibility of value-free research: "Feminists instead assert a commitment to changing the position of women and therefore society." It was with this background as a literacy teacher and sign language interpreter that I entered the field of deaf education.

As a hearing person fluent in Auslan, I negotiate from a position of both insider and outsider in my research and other work in Deaf education. I share membership in the same linguistic and professional community as most Australian teachers of deaf students; however, my fluency in Auslan is the defining characteristic that strengthens (or weakens) my insider status with deaf and hearing people. Although my lack of deafness and a Deaf family places me in the outer circles of the Deaf community, the authenticity of the accounts of Deaf participants in my research is positively influenced by my knowledge of their culture and language, as well as my interest in their political struggle. I share much the same identity with other hearing teachers who have acquired Auslan as a second language. I have embraced bilingual education, while acknowledging the position of power and privilege attached to the status of researcher.

CHAPTER 1

⁓

Power, Politics, and Education

ALTHOUGH A CENTRAL THEME of this book is the politics of language practices in deaf education, in my discussion I look beyond the issue of *access* to education to an analysis of the group and power relations that exist between Deaf and hearing people in schools, universities, and the broader community. Deaf people have traditionally been positioned, labeled, and constructed as "disabled" by educational and other powerful societal institutions. The level of support they receive is generally contingent on evidence and degree of "impairment"—another constructed term that takes its meaning from society's view of "ability" or "normality." In schools and universities, support for deaf students is provided on the basis of their "disability" or "impairment." The construction of deafness as a disability "has led to programs of the majority that aim to discourage Deaf children from participating in the Deaf World (programs such as oral education and cochlear implant surgery) and that aim to reduce the number of Deaf births, programs that are unethical from an ethnic group perspective" (Lane 2005).

Issues of power, control, and legitimacy are central to language practices in education. Deliberately or unwittingly, language practices are political acts that serve the interests of particular groups, often to the detriment of others. The way in which English is legitimized and perpetuated in deaf education is an example of the relationship between

1

language and power. Hearing educators, who are members of the dominant group, have traditionally established English as the legitimate language for use in education. Doing so maintains the unequal position of deaf people in society and further disempowers them as they struggle to gain access to education. Given the important ties between language and culture, denying students' native sign language in education devalues Deaf culture.

For researchers, poor outcomes in deaf education have fueled the debate over language practices and pedagogy. For decades, the international literature has made reference to the low level of education and poor literacy achievement of most deaf students. In the United States they generally attain the reading level of a fourth-grader. An Australian study of profoundly, prelingually deaf school-leavers in the mid-1990s found that deaf students were reading on average at the level of sixth-graders (Walker 1995). The explanation for their underachievement is debated by researchers and educators who express either of two viewpoints. The first maintains that the failure of deaf children in education is the result of their deafness and contends that the system strives to overcome this barrier as best it can with educational and medical intervention. The other view emphasizes the way in which deaf students have been educated and points to disabling pedagogy, rather than any disability in the child, as the cause of educational failure or underachievement. Supporting this second view is a large body of research and commentary on the benefits of native sign language as the first language and medium of instruction for deaf children (see Komesaroff 1998). Although not the first to promote bilingualism, Grosjean (1992) urged deaf people to realize they are bilingual and to take pride in it; their position as minority language bilinguals in a system that has failed to recognize their needs explains their failure in education.

The education of deaf people in Australia reflects a general trend toward mainstreaming in special education (Jenkinson 1997). With more than 80 percent of deaf or hearing-impaired students in Australia integrated into regular schools (Power 1994), the dominant approach has been to teach these students in English, spoken and/or signed. Senior managers in most state education agencies have generally been unwilling to become involved in the issue of language practices in deaf education, and there is little evidence that policymakers have considered the discrepancy between national policy (which recognizes deaf people as members of a cultural and linguistic minority; see Lo Bianco 1987) and educational policy and practices that directly or indirectly maintain English as the language of instruction. Despite increasing interest in native sign languages and a growing number of bilingual programs for deaf people, the policy and practices that dominate deaf education continue to reflect the values and interests of hearing professionals. Without proficiency in Auslan or knowledge of bilingual pedagogy, most teachers of deaf students have little option other than instructing in English. Deaf children are further disadvantaged by the significant underrepresentation of Deaf teachers in the profession.

The study that served as the impetus for this book (see chapter 2) investigated the ways in which teachers and other stakeholders in deaf education view language practices. Participants' comments have been critically analyzed in the context of language learning theory and viewed as a reflection of dominant or marginal discourse; in addition, their beliefs have been considered in relation to their position as members of the dominant or subordinate group. I have sought to scrutinize teachers' practices not by assessing the practices themselves as other Australian researchers have done (see Hyde and Power 1991, 1992; Hyde, Power, and Cliffe 1992; Leigh 1995) but by identifying the beliefs and structures that maintain those practices.

Issues of language, power, and identity are often absent from the discussion of educational methods, outcomes, and pedagogy. In the field of deafness, most research has been conducted by hearing people who have few or no cultural or linguistic ties to the Deaf community. Hearing educators commonly locate the failure (to speak, read, and write) in the child's deafness. In the introduction to her study of reading comprehension levels of deaf students in Australia, for example, Lyn Walker (1995, 6) claimed that "A hearing loss affects the child's acquisition of both receptive and expressive language. . . . With speech production problems, he or she may find it difficult to engage in conversation, thus not building up a rich language experience." A joint publication with Field Rickards (Walker and Rickards 1992), now dean of the Faculty of Education at the University of Melbourne, supports the conclusion reached by Des Power[1]: "Power (1975) was right in concluding that congenital deafness is a great barrier to learning." Power, who until his retirement headed the Deafness Studies Unit at Griffith University, Queensland, long held the view that deafness affects language development, literacy learning, and educational achievement: "It is widely recognized that it is exceptionally difficult for someone born significantly deaf or becoming so at an early age to develop the normal speech and language of the hearing/speaking community around them, or to reach normal standards of achievement in school (especially in subjects based mainly on language)" (Power 1996b, 12). Although acknowledging the role of Auslan in deaf people's lives ("for ease and fluency of communication among deaf people and its importance in developing identity as a Deaf person for family, social and recreational life as a Deaf adult" (ibid., 7), Power advocated the benefits of signed English and, at best, was noncommittal about any wide-scale future use of Auslan in education.

A cultural view of deafness does not confuse *language* with *speech* and challenges the assumption that deafness is a barrier to learning. This view holds true only if we assume that *communication, language,* and *normality* can be achieved only through *speech*. This position ignores the legitimacy of native sign languages and illustrates the way in which a minority language and its users can be rendered invisible (what, then, of the linguistic ability of Deaf people who acquire native sign language from birth, generally the children of Deaf adults?). Keeping native sign language out of the classroom or assigning it a subordinate role are examples of the way in which schools "put learners at risk by erecting barriers to learning" (Cambourne 1990, 291); Harlan Lane (1996) brands such practices as *audist* or *antideaf*:

> It is common for special educators to place blame for the academic underachievement of the Deaf child on the child and not on the school, as if the audist practices of the teacher and policies of the

---

1. In an oddly belated publication entitled "Auslan *Is* a Language" (Power 1996a), Power explains: "Thus they are not merely communication systems such as are used by some animals, but are indeed 'true languages.'"

school could not themselves be the primary reason for academic underachievement. The school, indeed the profession, insists that they are engaged simply in benevolent humanitarian practices in the face of overwhelming difficulties presented by the catastrophe of early childhood deafness.

The system of education for deaf people has been dominated by, and suited to, the needs of most hearing educators. Control has been maintained over deaf people through official language policies and a system that is structured to advantage hearing teachers:

> This arrangement minimizes what the teacher has to learn; the burden is not the teacher's to study the language of the students, nor to become familiar with their cultural and historical context. Moreover, students submerged in an alien language environment are submissive rather than autonomous; they recognize that their world and language have no place in the school and correctly assume that they are not valued. (ibid., 13)

The disabling structures present in deaf education reflect societal attitudes toward most linguistic minority groups. Children are especially vulnerable because "their instruction is organized through the medium of the majority languages in ways that contradict most scientific evidence" (Skutnabb-Kangas and Phillipson 1994, 106).

Viewing deaf children as members of a cultural and linguistic minority explains their educational underachievement in a system that considers them as having a disability. Like the members of other minority groups whose native language has been denied in education, their instruction through a second language reduces the support that a strong first language offers and takes away the central aspect of their cultural identity. Australian researchers Jan Branson and Don Miller (1991) have drawn a parallel between the underachievement of deaf students and that of aboriginal children; both groups have traditionally been taught by teachers who are linguistically and culturally different from them; as a result, they find themselves in a situation of social, cultural, and linguistic deprivation.

For deaf people, however, the lack of access to spoken information places them at a further disadvantage when native sign language is denied in the classroom. Deaf academic Breda Carty (cited in Vialle and Paterson 1996) similarly compares the experience of deaf students and aboriginal students and equates the removal of indigenous children from their homes and their placement in white foster families (known as the Stolen Generation) to the integration of deaf children in mainstream classrooms. She argues that mainstreaming threatens a deaf child's opportunity to develop a Deaf identity and that the ensuing search corresponds to that by the Stolen Generation for their lost identities. We have known for some time that minority students' success depends on how schools either reflect or counteract the power relations found in the wider community (Cummins 1994); yet, most deaf students continue to be deprived of their native language in education and thus are denied the opportunity for normal linguistic development.

An alternate approach (the basis of bilingual education) is for teachers to take into account their students' language, culture, and minority status. Among Australian teachers, the language practices in deaf education reveal the extent to which the exclusion of Auslan from the classroom is a deliberate denial of this minority group's language or the existence of other factors that have blocked its introduction. Significant personal and structural barriers to change indeed exist, not the least of which is the paucity of Deaf teachers and the general inability of teachers of deaf students to use Auslan. Oppression, however, may also exist in the absence of overt discrimination, although it is more likely to occur in the presence of one or more of the following conditions: exploitation, marginalization, powerlessness, cultural imperialism, and violence (Young 1992). Young's definition of cultural imperialism most closely resembles the conditions many Deaf people experience:

> Those living under cultural imperialism find themselves defined from the outside, positioned, and placed by a system of dominant meanings they experience as arising from elsewhere, from those with whom they do not identify and who do not identify with them. The dominant culture's stereotyped, marked, and inferiorized images of the group must be internalized by group members at least to the

degree that they are forced to react to behaviors of others that express or are influenced by those images. (ibid., 192)

Category Politics

To invoke the labels of Deaf and Hearing is to call up a web of relationships between what is central and what is peripheral, what is known and what is not known, and what is familiar and what is foreign. To talk of these terms is to offer a counterbalance between two large and imposing presences in Deaf people's lives—their own community and the community within which they must live, among hearing people.

—*Padden 1996, 89*

This book highlights the categories "disabled," "deaf," and "hearing" as sites of political debate, and it explores the consequences of this positioning. Dominant groups construct and position the "other," whether on the basis of gender, race, religion, sexuality, disability, or some other difference. Deaf people, like the members of other out-groups, are generally "located outside positions of power and influence" (Bacchi 1996, 11). Injustice has resulted not only from their economic marginalization and exploitation but also from disrespect, cultural domination, and lack of recognition (Fraser 1997). This perspective encourages the scrutiny of attitudes, values, and assumptions about social knowledge (Gilbert 1993).

Identity politics for deaf people enables them to challenge their positioning by the hearing majority and to explore the categories "deaf" and "hearing" (Padden and Humphries 1988). Perhaps by highlighting particular constructions and categories we can "denaturalize" these sites (see Butler 1992) by questioning previously taken-for-granted social constructs such as "deafness as disability." The deaf and hearing communities are "two large and imposing presences in Deaf people's lives" (Padden 1996, 89). The way in which one group defines (or is defined by) another raises issues of boundaries and exclusivity, as well as consequences. Rejecting the way they have been labeled and positioned, international and national Deaf leaders have called for self-determination and recognition of their rights as members of a cultural and linguistic group. At the same time, education programs, equity policies, and antidiscrimination laws in most countries define deafness as a disability and provide access to resources and support for deaf people on this basis.

In a 1998 interview, internationally renowned Deaf leader Carol-Lee Aquiline (the first general secretary of the World Federation of the Deaf) explained the implication of hearing people's dominance in education and the impact of the imposition of their "hearing" values on Deaf people:

> With a hearing teacher, no matter how much they care, they still never fully understand what it feels like to be deaf. So they'll never have the full ability to fully educate a deaf child in everything they need. They don't know what it is like to cut off their sense of hearing and experience the world visually. It is important for deaf children to have that. . . . Very, very few hearing teachers mix with the Deaf enough to become fluent in Auslan and communicate comfortably. (Komesaroff 1998, 238)

By their very ability to hear, hearing teachers cannot provide deaf students with a fully positive model of deafness; deaf students internalize the inferior status ascribed to them by a hearing, English-speaking world in which their language is largely ignored. In the same interview, Aquiline related an incident that occurred in the mid-1990s when, in her role as president of the Australian Association of the Deaf, she was visiting schools to talk to deaf children about the achievements of Deaf people. She said, "We are going into schools and saying to kids, 'Hey, I'm here. I'm Deaf and it's good! Look at what I'm doing, traveling the world and so on.' I think the role-modeling thing is very important" (ibid., 242). She was telling the children about the achievements of Deaf people—a lawyer, an Olympic athlete, teachers, and other Deaf professionals—when she noticed a young deaf boy looking at her with a puzzled expression, so she asked him what he wanted to do in the future:

> He thought for a bit and then said, "Maybe a panel beater or something like that." And I said, "You mean you love cars?" And he said,

"No, not really. . . . The teacher told me that's all I can do." He actually said that: "The teacher told me that's all I can do!" I just felt churned up inside. Where's education going wrong! It's supposed to open doors, not slam them shut and lock them behind. (ibid., 239)

The graphic contrasts in this story with its binary images of "deaf child" and "hearing adult," "manual labor" versus "professional activity," and an "open door" as opposed to one that is "slammed shut and locked from behind" are vivid.

One way to address the marginality of Deaf people is to recognize the ways in which the dominant group has positioned them and the consequences of categorizing them as having a disability. If we are to have an inclusive society—"a society built upon ideals of social justice where participation and success are irrespective of 'race,' gender, socio-economic status, ethnicity, age and disability so that disadvantage is not reproduced" (Nunan, Rigmor, and McAusland 2000)—we need to listen more closely to those who are different from the majority. Labeling deaf people as "disabled" runs counter to their cultural values and efforts toward self-determination. Access and equity policies may allow students with disabilities entry into mainstream institutions but often leave them unaltered and fall short of considering critical reform agendas (Rizvi and Lingard 1996, 21): "It is not sufficient for these students simply to have access—their engaged participation is necessary; it should be not merely symbolic but real." Constructing Deaf people as individuals with a disability ignores their status as minority language bilinguals— something Ladd (2003) calls their "positive biology."

Education providers (such as universities that are aware of the debate over category politics) may find themselves entangled in a policy dilemma. Legislation for equal rights names the social groups that institutions must provide access to (Bacchi 1996). In so doing, Deaf people are labeled as having a disability. Bacchi suggests that one solution is for those represented in a category to be "present in [sufficient] numbers to debate its uses" (ibid.). The limited number of Deaf people in educational institutions in Australia restricts their opportunity to discuss such issues of marginality.

The idea that Deaf people can be added to existing institutions without disturbing the broader political agenda is no longer acceptable. Yet, Deaf people are confronted with "discursive marginality" in much the same way that women are—in other words, "not a state that represents 'men's interests' as against women's, but government conducted as if men's interests are the only ones that exist" (Pringle and Watson 1992, 57). Similarly, "hearing interests" are generally not represented as *opposing* Deaf interests; rather, powerful institutions such as schools and universities are conducted as if hearing interests are the *only* ones that exist.

CHAPTER 2

Politically Active Research

Those of us working in this arena need to understand that the politics of language is always about more than language. We need to understand ourselves and the internalized oppression that tells us English and hearing people are superior to ASL [American Sign Language] and Deaf people. We need to understand how this is at work in us and change ourselves and our attitudes while we struggle to change the system.

—*Kannapell 1990*

THE THEMES OF POWER, politics, and the struggle for self-determination among Deaf people thread through this book. Despite recognition of the linguistic legitimacy of Auslan in the late 1980s, the language and culture of Deaf people are still routinely denied to most deaf children through educational policy, language practices, and, more recently, medical intervention. Attention to the political nature of language practices in deaf education is critical if changes are to be made to the power relations between deaf people and hearing people. From my own research (Komesaroff 1998), I have found that Australian teachers of deaf students, policymakers, Deaf leaders, and parents of deaf children hold competing beliefs and attitudes about language practices in deaf education. Furthermore, hearing teachers and a "hearing perspective" of deafness have long dominated deaf education in Australia. Before we examine current practices, a review of the history of deaf education in Australia is in order.

Formal education for deaf people in Australia began in 1860, when the first schools for deaf students were established in Sydney and Melbourne (Crickmore 1995). Until 1879 teachers instructed by means of the "manual method"—sign language and fingerspelling (Stevens, Smitt, Thomas, and Wilson 1995). In 1876 the "pure oral method" (speech and lipreading) was tried with a small number of students, although the management committee for the Victorian institution did not favor this approach. The events at the Milan Congress in 1880, however, were to change the education of deaf children in Australia, as well as in other countries around the world.

At the international meeting in Milan, teachers of deaf students had voted for the use of the pure oral method over the "combined method" (the use of speech and signs together) in their belief that the use of signs would have the "disadvantage of injuring articulation and lip-reading and the precision of ideas" (Tarra 1880, 64). It was widely believed that signs represented a limited range of ideas and hindered the development of thought and reasoning (Ewing and Ewing 1938). When delegates voted to ban sign language from deaf education and proclaimed the superiority of speech over sign, the outcome was ensured by the general exclusion of deaf people from the vote (only one of the 164 delegates was deaf; see Lane 1984). Efforts to teach Deaf people to speak have persisted throughout history, but after the Milan Congress, Deaf teachers were removed from schools, and sign language was generally outlawed. The dominance of oralism persisted well into the twentieth century.

By 1881 the Victorian school had introduced the combined method. Although the use of this method continued throughout the early 1900s (MacDougall 1988), in 1905 the headmaster reported that speech and lipreading dominated classroom communication and that signs and fingerspelling were used sparingly (Crickmore 1995). In the 1930s (and perhaps earlier), the "Rochester method" (in which every word is fingerspelled; see Johnston 1989) was also used. In 1950 a visit from British oralists Irene Ewing and Alex Ewing sparked the fervor for oral education in Australia. Highly critical of the Australian schools they visited, the Ewings called for the establishment of oral-only institutions. A year after the publication of their report to the Commonwealth Office of Education, an oral school for deaf children was founded in Victoria. The same year, Queensland, which had previously made use of the combined or Rochester methods, instituted a purely oral system (Burch and Hyde 1984). At the Fifth Triennial Conference of the Australian Association of Teachers of the Deaf in 1953, Australian teachers rejected sign language in favor of oral methods and declared that fingerspelling and gestures were outmoded (Branson and Miller 1989).

In the 1970s Signed English was developed in Australia. This system grew out of the combined method and the Australian Sign Language Development Project, the first attempt by educators to standardize and direct sign language use in Australia. "Eliminating ambiguity and establishing one meaning only for each controlled movement" were cited as the goals of the project (Jeanes 1970, 43). The production of signs in English word order, with fingerspelling, was expected to give signing "grammatical construction": "Deaf children left to their own devices will communicate. However, this communication is not our socially accepted language. The use of Combined Method is an attempt by some educators to make this communication into a grammatical, meaningful language, to extend deaf children's horizons and direct their lives to some purpose" (ibid., 44).

When several Auslan signs were in use for a particular concept (such as anger), one sign was selected. Verb endings were added by fingerspelling after the root sign (such as ANGER-E-D), new signs were invented for irregular verbs, and whole words were fingerspelled (MacDougall 1988). By 1974 many teachers of deaf students were concerned about the lack of a one-to-one correspondence between English and the native sign lexicon. A single Auslan sign was often used to express the meaning of more than one English word; occasionally, compound signs (the combination of two or more signs) were used to represent a single word in English (Jeanes and Reynolds 1981), such as DON'T-KNOW and THINK-TRUE ("believe"). Teachers who were working with deaf students became convinced of the educational advantage of combining fingerspelling with signs to represent English syntax (ibid.), and in 1977 the following guidelines for signing in English were adopted: "Only one sign would be used to represent the multiple meanings of an English word, additional signs would be invented for English words represented by the same sign in Auslan, and compound words in English would be represented by two separate signs" (MacDougall 1988).

Under this system, for example, only one sign was to be used for "blind" ("unable to see"), "blind" ("window blind"), and "blind" ("blind drunk"); individual signs were invented for the English words "mend," "fix," and "repair," and "bathroom" was signed as BATH + ROOM.[1] Signs were altered if they obscured the face, an indication that Signed English was intended to be used in conjunction with speech and lipreading. Teachers expected Signed English to provide an accurate representation of English syntax and thereby to assist deaf children with reading and writing. They were careful at the time to indicate that their intention was *not* to change Deaf people's native language but to improve deaf children's communicative competence and English abilities.

Systems such as the one developed by Australian educators are known generically as *contrived systems* and are devised by committees of mostly hearing educators who borrow signs from the national sign language and invent new signs to represent tense and irregular parts of speech (Lane, Hoffmeister, and Bahan 1996). They reflect the view that a code that is based on spoken language is superior to native sign language and can overcome what are seen as "deficiencies" in the native sign language. There are conflicting accounts of the extent to which deaf people supported or opposed the development of Signed English in Australia. Leigh (1995, 280), for example, reported "considerable early acceptance of, and involvement in, the development and use of the system by Deaf people." Deaf academic Breda Carty (1994), however, says that such claims fail to take account the issues of the power differential between hearing teachers and Deaf people. She maintains that the Deaf community had little information about how Signed English was going to be

---

1. During my observation of teachers using Signed English, I also saw BUTTER + FLY (for "butterfly") and even PASS + SPORT (for "passport").

used and that hearing educators showed utter disregard for their native language:

> It is often claimed that hearing teachers and Deaf people were equal partners in the process [of developing Signed English], and superficially it may look as if this was true—but it wasn't true at all. The process was undertaken by two unevenly balanced groups of people. One group, the majority, consisted of native users of a powerful and widely used language, invested with all of the decision-making powers in the education of deaf children. The other group . . . [consisted of] minority, native users of an unrecognized language, with no decision-making power in the education of Deaf children. The underlying premise was that the language of this minority was inexact and inadequate (at least for teaching), indeed not a real language, but that it could somehow be whipped into shape if it was entrusted to the "experts." (ibid., 19)

The withdrawal of support by the deaf members of the development committee and the committee's decision to proceed no matter what is an indication of the teachers' belief in "their authority not only over education but over signing as a mode" (Branson and Miller 1993, 29).

Now, in the early twenty-first century, deaf education in Australia is in a state of flux. A large group of educators is still vigorously pursuing oral education, which has been further buoyed by the dominance of children with cochlear implants (CIs) in this country. The belief in oralism and the removal of sign language from the educational and home environment of implanted deaf children are generally supported by the conservative views held by most of the CI professionals. Teachers of deaf students who support the use of English (spoken and/or signed) continue to stymie (directly or indirectly) deaf children's access to native sign language. For more than ten years, parents of deaf children who have requested Auslan as the language of instruction have met with resistance. Complaints against schools and school authorities have been vigorously defended in the courts, court rulings have in at least one case been appealed, and teachers of deaf students (TODs) have gone on record to defend practices that exclude Auslan. In doing so, their views more closely represent those of their oralist colleagues than the Deaf people and their allies who are campaigning for systemic change (see chapter 5).

Politically Active Research

This study of local educational settings exposes and scrutinizes the extant power relationships. My research identifies a theoretical and pedagogical gulf between educators who defended established practices (the use of spoken or Signed English) and those who advocated change (the introduction of bilingual programs).[2] Arguments on both sides deal with issues of cultural membership, theories of language and literacy, and claims about educational achievement.

No lens through which we view the world is culturally neutral; it always privileges one cultural group over another (Fraser 1997). Therefore, educational researchers must acknowledge the particular lens they are using and recognize what it includes and excludes. In doing so, they will be able to challenge assumed knowledge. In the context of deaf education, it means resisting the view of language as politically neutral or dealing only with issues of individual ability or deficit (in contrast to socially and culturally constructed deficit). Thus, the notion of "deafness as disability" is called into question, and attention is drawn to the deficit construction of deaf people that pervades government policy, legislation, and educational practice. When the debate in deaf education is repositioned from *communication* (the use of speech or signs) to *language* (the use of English or Auslan), schools are exposed as sites of dominant hearing ideologies. The study of language in the real-world context of schools for deaf children has identified the way in which many of these students' teachers view communication as linguistically or politically neutral.

In deaf education, too little evidence exists of the pluralist ideal of providing for a "multiplicity of voices" (McQuail 1987, cited in Lewis

---

2. This research has also been used as evidence in federal court cases and as the basis of witness statements in cases brought by parents of deaf children against educational authorities for alleged discrimination (see chapter 5).

2001, 101). An acceptance of diversity may be implied by including or holding a dialogue with "the other" while ensuring no loss of self-interest or control and conceding little in the way of structural change (Munshi and McKie 2001). Deaf education has been dominated by a reductionist view of diversity as "different modes of communication." In English-speaking nations, spoken English, written English, or Signed English has dominated the education of deaf people. This has been done largely to the exclusion or marginalization of native sign languages.

In Australia and many other English-speaking nations, English dominates the classroom in deaf education. This occurs despite government recognition of the legitimacy of native sign languages such as Australian Sign Language (Lo Bianco 1987) and appeals from Deaf leaders, who point out that the policies of their organizations advise the use of the native sign language as the language of instruction and first language for deaf children (Australian Association of the Deaf 1997; World Federation of the Deaf 1993).

The Research Study

In conducting my research, I interviewed TODs and observed classroom lessons in three different schools, which I call schools 1, 2, and 3. I assumed an active participant-observer role and wrote my field notes during or soon after each observation. At schools 1 and 2 I interviewed teachers and observed classes during biweekly or monthly visits over an eight-month period. I visited school 3 every two weeks throughout the school year and spent two or three days each time because of the school's distance from my home. These visits heightened my involvement in the community. I had access to students, teachers, and parents inside and outside regular school hours; I attended night meetings of the parents' council; and I interacted with the deaf students at the dormitory in which I stayed. This maximized the opportunity to collect rich data and actively contribute to the direction and outcomes of the study.

The goal of asking teachers of deaf students to take part in a study of language practices was to engage them in a political discussion about education and issues of power. Although my bilingual status may have dissuaded some participants from taking part in the research, it had the opposite effect on the teachers at school 3, which became the main case study. There, teachers not only agreed to participate but also sought my active involvement to assist the school in its investigation of bilingual deaf education. Considering the introduction of Auslan and bilingual practices, the study was viewed as an opportunity for the staff members to gather information and enlist support that were otherwise inaccessible. This clearly influenced the choice of research methodology for this site, shaped as it is by the purpose of the study and the research questions. I adopted an "educative" research paradigm for school 3 (Gitlin, Siegel, and Boru 1993), entered into dialogue with the teachers, parents, students, and administrators, and responded to their requests for information. I took an active role in the school's consideration of change, explained the theoretical underpinnings of bilingual pedagogy to the parents and teachers, and modeled bilingual practices. A significant factor in the change that ultimately took place was the teachers' opportunity to see *their* children or students interacting with Auslan speakers in *their* homes or classrooms.

The entire study involved interviews with fifty participants—teachers in the three case study schools, parents of students in school 3, principals and coordinators of schools or facilities for deaf children, organization representatives, and other key stakeholders in deaf education. The principals and coordinators of all of the facilities or schools for deaf children in Victoria were also invited to be interviewed; six agreed to do so, including two retired principals from oral schools who were selected to include as wide a range of views as possible. Five managers from state and regional offices of the Department of Education (DOE), the national president of the association of TODs, the president of a state association of parents of deaf children, and four Deaf leaders representing state and national organizations of Deaf people were also interviewed. Other stakeholders included a senior lecturer who was responsible for training teachers of deaf children, four parents who had taken legal action against a school for deaf students, a cochlear implant surgeon, an international writer and researcher in the field of deafness and deaf education, and a Deaf TOD working in the tertiary sector.

A little more than half of the participants in the study were qualified TODs. These teachers were generally very experienced; eighteen of the twenty-six teachers had more than ten years' experience in deaf education. Almost half had no experience in regular education. Most of them instructed in English (spoken or signed) or produced simultaneously (Total Communication, or TC, which is the use of signs, fingerspelling, speech, and residual hearing). Five had native skills or were fluent in Auslan, and three had some or moderate skills in Auslan; they cannot, however, be considered a representative sample of the wider profession.

Most of the participants were female and hearing. Of the eighteen male participants, half held leadership positions in the DOE. Seven participants were deaf, just under half of whom were leaders of organizations representing Deaf people; no deaf participants were employed as principals or coordinators of schools or facilities or held other leadership positions in the DOE. The language skills of the participants (other than the TODs) generally reflected their cultural status as Deaf or hearing people. The Deaf participants who were organization representatives or parents of deaf children were native or fluent users of Auslan. With the exception of one TOD (the child of deaf adults), English was the first language of all of the hearing participants. Other than some TODs, no other hearing participants were fluent in Auslan; two of the parents of deaf children had some skills in Auslan, and one other hearing participant had skills in another native sign language.

The primary data for this study were interview transcripts. Interviews were conducted with all of the participants; the participants in the case study schools were interviewed up to three times, and two group meetings were conducted with the parents in the main case study. Interviews were semistructured and averaged fifty minutes in length. The participants received a transcript of each interview soon after the discussion was completed, and they were invited to make additional comments or alterations.

The interview transcripts were analyzed using a qualitative data analysis software program known as NUDIST (see Richards and Richards 1991).[3] The program allowed me to index substantial text-based data.

---

3. The acronym NUDIST stands for nonnumerical unstructured data indexing, searching, and theorizing; the program is now available as QSR N6.

All of the interview transcripts were entered into the software program, and I began the analysis by coding the text into categories. I then defined and constructed an initial set of categories from prior theory and logic. After some experimentation with a few interviews, the key categories and subcategories became clear; these were changed, augmented, and refined as I analyzed more data. The main categories were the following:

1. Auslan
2. Signed English
3. oral education
4. bilingual education
5. training
6. change
7. beliefs
8. barriers
9. current issues

As an example of the subcategories, comments about bilingual education were further indexed as positive influences, negative beliefs, general, or establishment of bilingual education. Two further levels of categorization were created.

Text was selected and allocated to these categories based on my analysis of the central meanings found in the data. After indexing all of the interview transcripts in this way, I generated reports that showed the categories to which text had been indexed across an individual transcript or groups of transcripts. By producing reports in this way, I found that key areas of interest clearly emerged. These prompted discussion in subsequent interviews and enabled me to identify the categories to which no data had been indexed. I used these reports to discuss emerging themes from previous interviews or to question teachers on issues that other participants raised. The reports on each site generated a broad view of the school community.

The selection of narratives from the interview transcripts for analysis and inclusion in the final report is a political act that either gives voice to or silences particular statements the participants made. Qualitative researchers select and edit certain comments by participants. Selected for their relevance to the central research questions, these "pieces of narrative evidence" (Fine 1994, 22) become interwoven with the research report. In this study I was primarily interested in the participants' changing views of deafness, language practices, and pedagogy.

Opposing Philosophies

Approaches to communication with deaf people have long been contested. The competing paradigms of speech and sign language have traditionally split the field of deaf education, leaving oral education on one side and the use of signing (whether contrived or native) on the other. The beliefs that underlie teachers' language practices demonstrate particular assumptions about Deaf people and their language. Their comments illustrate two patterns of attitudes that I call a hearing worldview and a Deaf worldview. Of the slightly more than eight hundred teachers working in this field in 1998, 97.4 percent were hearing, and less than 1 percent of the deaf or hearing-impaired teachers were native or fluent users of Auslan (Komesaroff 1998). It is not surprising, therefore, that teachers who reject bilingual education lack proficiency in Auslan (supporters of oral-only methods were unable to use any form of sign language, whether native or contrived). In recent years, the focus has shifted to the language, rather than the mode, of communication used in deaf education: "I mean, if as teachers of the deaf we don't acknowledge that deaf kids, profoundly, prelingually deaf kids, have a language problem, then we've got a lot to learn as far as deaf education is concerned" (Participant 16).

A Hearing Worldview

Many educators who support oralism or Total Communication share common views of the place of English in the classroom. The set of beliefs I characterize here as a hearing worldview are commonly held by teachers who support the dominant-group language, English (spoken and/or signed), for instruction. This position eliminates or marginalizes the use of Auslan in the classroom:

- English is the most appropriate language for education.
- Deaf children require a variety of communication methods.
- Language policy is chiefly determined by parents.
- Students' failure or underachievement is a result of their deafness.
- Deaf students' difficulty in acquiring literacy results from a *lack* of exposure to English; therefore, they require *more* exposure to English.
- English is more structured, more formal, and more appropriate than native sign language for use in education.
- Native sign language, if considered, is appropriate only for Deaf children from Deaf families, for informal language use, for use in the Deaf community, or as a last resort if other methods have failed. Students can acquire Auslan informally at a later age if they decide to enter the Deaf community.

Oral educators expect deaf students to succeed through methods that rely on speech and hearing. However, TC educators believe that oral education has failed deaf children and that the addition of signs is necessary for their success (a view that bilingual educators also hold). Some oral teachers believe that deaf children should not be taught sign language because few hearing people knew Auslan. Others believe that hearing teachers and parents should not be expected to learn Auslan and that speech is essential to acquiring language and attaining success in education and the wider community: "I like the fact that they can come back here and they can make themselves understood and they can converse really freely with a whole range of hearing people here or they can go and hold down a job without having to have an interpreter or they can have a hearing girlfriend or boyfriend if they so desire."

This teacher, who was the coordinator of a deaf facility, described her students as successful when they made friendships and found employment "without [the use of] an interpreter"; they were students whose speech was so good "you could barely know that they were deaf." She took pride in their ability to interact in the hearing world and judged them on their ability to perform as hearing, speaking individuals. She acknowledged their struggle to acquire oral skills but believed that her students, as adults, would think the effort was worthwhile. She dismissed the contradictory evidence from many deaf people and believed their criticism was the result of political pressure from the Deaf community:

> I know the kids who have gone through here have made public statements about oral/aural settings, and yet privately, to me, they don't say those things; in fact, they say the opposite. . . . *A lot of the time the very skills that are enabling them to articulate the sort of feelings that they have come from what they've gone through.* And yet, look, I don't for one second say that this is an easy road. This is a bloody hard row to hoe! There is no doubt about it, absolutely, absolutely shockingly difficult! But I think that the rewards at the end can be really significant (emphasis added).
>
> I don't expect kids here—where they are in Grade 5, Grade 6—are going to have the same facility with English [as hearing kids] either. But as long as they are moving forward and they're not too far behind and they . . . are making themselves understood and they're not floundering in the classroom, then I figure that's pretty good.

She believes Auslan is inappropriate for deaf children from hearing families and endorses the approach of always beginning with oral education:

> Unless it was deaf parents, I would always explore the auditory modality as early and as much as possible because it is the way most of us have learned language, without having to have it taught to us, and advances in technology have made it possible for more children to get more of that [auditory] signal and therefore learn rather than be taught language. So I'd always explore that fully first before I did anything else. (Participant 6)

While recognizing the difficulty facing parents without skills in Auslan or knowledge of deafness, this participant fails to consider the situation of the deaf child who is unable to gain access to the language or culture of the hearing family. Her comments also fail to acknowledge the place of subcultures that exist within the wider community and exclude deaf children of hearing parents from Deaf culture.

A Deaf Worldview

The beliefs of all of the participants who viewed native sign language and Deaf culture as central to the success of deaf students in education can be characterized as a Deaf worldview. This position was taken by the Deaf teachers, Deaf leaders, and bilingual educators who were interviewed. These participants voiced their dissatisfaction with teacher education, criticized teachers' current language practices, and expressed anger at the control that hearing people continue to exercise over deaf people and their education. The participants based their advocacy of Auslan and bilingual education on current language-learning theory, which points to the importance of a strong, accessible language by means of which deaf children can acquire English as a second language.

Moreover, they endorsed the use of Auslan to teach English literacy by contrasting and comparing the features of both languages. Given the limited access to Auslan that most deaf children (who, incidentally, are born into hearing families) face, bilingual educators consider this to be another reason for the language and culture of Deaf people to be a central part of education. In the Deaf worldview, it is illogical to deny deaf children access to linguistic and educational development through their native sign language simply because their parents are not deaf. One teacher said, "We are doing them a disservice if we don't at least let them know that there is another world out there that they can belong to." The success of bilingual education requires teachers not only to be able to communicate with deaf people but also to have a positive attitude toward them, their language, and their culture. It also entails "an attitude of acceptance, not just tolerating the existence of this other language, but embracing it, taking full advantage of it" (Davies 1994, 112).

The beliefs that characterize a Deaf worldview include the following:

- Auslan should be endorsed as the language of instruction and developed as deaf children's first language.

- With a strong language base in native sign language, deaf children will learn English as a second language through reading and writing.
- Given access to Auslan, deaf children will acquire age-appropriate language skills.
- Spoken and Signed English lack meaning for deaf children and are linguistically and visually confusing.
- Signed English offends the Deaf community and needs to be un-learned by deaf people if they wish to join the community of culturally and linguistically Deaf adults.

Participants with a Deaf worldview rejected the positioning of English as the language of instruction. They harshly criticized oral education (as did most TC educators) and rejected Signed English or TC approaches. A bias toward speech and oral methods was considered to have failed deaf children. Those with personal experience of oral education (as a teacher or student) criticized the fervor with which oral educators impose spoken English and recounted stories of students who had failed to acquire language through this method. In addition, Deaf leaders were highly critical of the entrenched practices in deaf education:

> If you were blunt, you would say, "Well, you've been doing it wrong for the last ten years!" It would break anyone's heart to know that you've done a lousy job or been taught how to do a lousy job without knowing it! (Participant 8)

> I think it is human nature not to want to admit you are wrong, that you have been doing the wrong thing for the past twenty years. That's part of the problem; it is pride. Part of the problem is their attitude. They are still very strong about hearing and speaking being better, and that attitude is still there. They don't want to give that up, that dream about making deaf children hear and speak well. (Participant 7)

A parents' organization representative challenged the oral educators' be-lief that they were serving parents' wishes by encouraging them to use speech with their children. Instead, this parent claimed that educational and medical professionals were advising them to persist with speech and to set it as the primary goal of education. General practitioners, she said, assumed speech was the best—and perhaps only—option for a deaf child and steered parents toward oral education. Oral educators then perpetuated the parents' desire for their child to speak and failed to dispel the myth that they could do so.

A significant number of teachers (fifteen), including several with many years' experience using TC, criticized Signed English. Unlike those with a hearing worldview (who lacked skills in the language they criticized and were able to teach only through English), only two of the teachers who rejected English as the language of instruction were native Auslan users. Most were still developing Auslan skills or had yet to begin acquiring them. In calling for a bilingual approach to deaf education, these teachers understood that they needed to learn a new language. Their rejection of Signed English was based on the lack of emphasis on visual meaning, the linguistic and visual confusion it created, its inability to function as a complete and accessible language, and the difficulty in producing and receiving simultaneous communication. The dearth of systematic research to show that Signed English facilitated language acquisition was yet another reason given by one participant: "It would be truly astonishing if it [Signed English] did work because it is so counter to everything we know about language and psycholinguistics" (Participant 28). Furthermore, a bilingual educator pointed to the confusion created by mixing two languages and stated that the popularity of Signed English was due to the ease with which a hearing adult could learn it: "My opinion of Signed English . . . is that it shouldn't be used, and it's a waste of time, quite frankly. It totally destroys the whole philosophy that English and . . . Auslan are separate and they should remain separate. . . . I really don't think that it has a place at all" (Participant 27).

The participants believed that parents should be provided with an opportunity to learn Auslan instead of being led to spoken or Signed English by hearing professionals. They also believed that disabling pedagogy accounted for the poor results in deaf education and that deaf children need positive deaf role models to help them acquire the language and culture of the Deaf community: "The child is deaf, so Deaf culture makes a lot of sense, rather than trying to make the deaf person fit into a hearing world" (Participant 15). A key structural barrier to the wider use of Auslan in deaf education, however, was the lack of consideration of bilingual education by policymakers in state educational agencies. In the late 1990s, for example, policymakers in the Victorian Department of Education recognized Auslan as a language other than English (LOTE) and thus an addition to the curriculum, but they were not aware of its use in bilingual deaf education. Managers at the state and regional level also indicated their unwillingness to become involved in the issue of language practices in this field.

Cultural Identities

"Surgeons have made the claim that a Deaf child is not yet a member of the Deaf-World and thus a program of implanting Deaf children should not be viewed as undermining that ethnic minority" (Cohen 1994). In fact, these doctors imply that Deaf people should mind their own business because young deaf children of hearing parents are not culturally Deaf. Since much turns on this point, it is worth considering the logic of how we make cultural assignments.

Three possible premises emerge: An infant belongs to no culture at all until a certain age or stage of development; an infant "inherits" its parents' culture at birth; or an infant has the cultural affiliation it will normally acquire. It is a fact that children are launched at the moment of birth onto a trajectory that, depending on their makeup and environment, will normally lead them to master a particular language and culture. It is this potential in a newborn Native American child, for example, that leads us to say that the child *is* Native American (not *will be*), although the child has not yet acquired the language and culture that go with that cultural affiliation. In making this attribution we do not ask first about the parents' culture. Their physical makeup and ethnicity, while usually consonant with their child's, do not decide the child's cultural assignment; it is the child's makeup that does. With adoptive parents or even a surrogate mother, a child with a Native American constitution would be called Native American. Thus, a program of adopting such infants into Caucasian homes would be guilty of undermining Native American culture, and its proponents could not deny this fact on the grounds that the children had not yet learned that culture and language.

Similarly, a newborn Deaf child *is* culturally Deaf, and a program of implanting Deaf children does indeed undermine that cultural identity. To see the link more clearly, imagine that the program had one hundred percent success with implants; the result would be no Deaf children and therefore no Deaf World. The Deaf infant may not yet have acquired the language and culture that are, given its makeup, its natural right and heritage, which it will prize as an adult (since most people who are born Deaf do), but the child's life trajectory is surely headed there. This child will use vision almost exclusively and will communicate visually, not aurally. The child may have biological parents who are hearing, but this child is not a hearing person either in principle, as we have seen, or in practice. As a matter of practice, if the parents cannot communicate fluently with their child, they will be severely hampered in teaching the child their language and culture, and the child will never be able to acquire them naturally—without instruction—as a hearing child would. However adept hearing parents may be, they cannot model Deaf adulthood, only hearing adulthood, and a child who relies primarily on vision will never develop into a hearing person, not even remotely. The parents, on the other hand, will never be culturally Deaf. Thus, uncommon as it may be among other cultures, Deaf children and their parents very often do not share the same cultural membership.

One participant said she would like to use Auslan but that it would be "unnecessary" and "a waste of time" learning it. The language she used to describe Auslan focused on its surface level—"beautiful . . . terrific . . . gorgeous"—without mentioning its linguistic and cultural value, depth, and complexity. Asked about the possibility of providing education by means of Auslan-using Deaf teachers, she said, "All deaf educators? Well, you won't see it here. . . . You wouldn't see it in a setting like this, which is a *normally hearing* school. I wouldn't think so, and the reason that I say that is so many—much of the time that we're in the class, we have to be the *ears for the kids*. So if you've got somebody who's deaf and trying to support a deaf student in a classroom where—it wouldn't work" (emphasis added). (Participant 16)

In her self-defined role as the "ears for the kids," this participant excluded the possibility that deaf people could be employed in deaf education and saw little need to redefine the relationship between schools and the Deaf community, as well as between teachers and deaf students. Just as she had ignored their criticism of oral education, this teacher also dismissed Deaf people's stated preference for instruction through Auslan as political. Her view of bilingual education was that it was risky and unproven and might not succeed with deaf children:

> I can't afford to let a generation of deaf kids . . . be guinea pigs. . . . It's got to be well researched, well documented, and if it's not working, then there have got to be good educational reasons why it is changed. You don't persevere with something that isn't working because it is politically correct.
>
> Yeah, well, I think there's a fair bit of politics in that, and I can understand that. . . . What I don't want to see is a situation where kids are being sacrificed on the altar of some kind of sociopolitical argument. So once you start confusing educational decisions with sociopolitical things, I think there's a danger that that could be happening, and possibly the educational debate is hijacked by people who aren't educators, and that worries me. (Participant 16)

This participant expressed her attitude toward Auslan with emotion-laden words such as *sacrificed, danger,* and *hijacked.* She accused Deaf people of politicizing the debate with false argument and involving people who are not educators. In her view, only *Deaf* people have politics, ignoring her own political stance. The views of deaf people are not seriously considered because they lack teaching qualifications. Similar claims of politicizing the curriculum have been made against other oppressed groups such as women and people of color (Fine 1994).

Total Communication was expected to provide students with a variety of approaches, although the only language presented is generally English. Teachers described deaf students as having "individual linguistic needs," and they reported that they used whatever method worked for the child. They believed that, in this way, they were "fitting the method to the child." Teachers talked about communication, making meaning, and interaction but rarely about *language*. They often used the generic expression *signing* to describe their communication practices, which is a reference to a communication *mode*, not the *language* they used (English).

If Auslan were to be used at all, it was regarded as a tool for communication rather than a language in its own right. The assumption that English is more structured than Auslan indicates a lack of linguistic knowledge of sign languages. The view that deaf children from hearing families are not culturally or linguistically Deaf is used to legitimize the use of English and perpetuates the exclusion of Auslan from the classroom. Participant 6 offered the following comments on this attitude:

> I think as far as providing structural language for the kids, there's a very strong need for Signed English. Some kids won't pick that up just through reading and writing; they need a structure to hang it on, to see where it all fits into place, and I still think that's vital for an English language side of things, a formalized English language.
>
> If they've experienced how English operates in all its subtleties and all its nuances and all its vagueness often as a language, to be able to experience that and to see it in operation and then relate that to a literary sense, you can't deny the value of that. Well, *I* can't deny the value of that.
>
> I believe that the clients of a program or a school are the family, not the child; it is desirable for children to learn the language of their culture, and, to me, for a deaf child in a hearing family, the Deaf community is not their culture.
>
> I think the culture of a baby is their family. . . . I don't believe there is any other culture where we expect a family to bring their child up in a culture that they don't share any values with at all. . . . I think that placing the expectation that this deaf baby belongs to this Deaf community and you learn that community's language to teach the child, to share a culture that you don't know anything about is just an impossible situation. (Participant 6, 165)

A recurring theme among the participants with a hearing worldview was the belief that deaf students' difficulties at school were the result of limited communication in the home. They expected deaf children to succeed in education when there was communication at home, regardless of the form it took. These participants believed that instructing deaf children in English served the parents' wishes, and any failure among deaf children was the result of either lack of communication at home or the child's language and learning disabilities: "Yes, their behavior was terrible. Why was that? Yes, their literacy was terrible, but why was that? Their learning skills were terrible; their concentration was terrible; why was that? And it always seemed to come back to communication. Well, we're communicating here, so we decided it was at the family level." (Participant 20)

Teachers who supported the use of TC described English as "structural" and "formalized," with "subtleties" and "nuances." Their preference for Signed English was based on the view that Auslan "lacked formality" and "structure" and that, to learn English, students needed to "see English on the hands." They expected Signed English to make spoken language accessible to deaf children despite the well-documented account of the inconsistent and inaccurate model of English that simultaneous communication provides (for an Australian study, see Giroux 1992).

Support for Auslan was restricted to its introduction as a language other than English, and teachers expressed little doubt that Signed English would continue to be the language of instruction in their classrooms. The inclusion of Auslan as an LOTE has brought increased access to Auslan for many deaf students. However, access to Auslan for only an hour or two a week may do little to redress the systemic denial of a language. Deaf students are exposed to Auslan when they enter specialist classes, which are generally taught by deaf staff who are qualified as LOTE teachers. In TC settings, they return to instruction in Signed English, generally by hearing teachers who are not fluent in Auslan.

Many teachers believe that Signed English is easier than Auslan for hearing people to acquire and that teachers cannot be expected to speak or instruct in a language that is foreign to them. The principal of a school for deaf children that introduced Auslan as a language other than English in 1997 believes the move threatened some teachers and heightened their fear that Auslan would take over as the language of instruction. He assured them that their fears were groundless and that English would continue to be used in the classroom. If a child used an Auslan sign outside the LOTE class, he told his teachers to say, for example, "Oh, I'm sorry, but that's Auslan; [in] Signed English we use that sign for 'giraffe.' . . . That's the sign we use in this classroom" (Participant 30). He paralleled the situation in which teachers were unable to understand their students' use of Auslan with that of a teacher whose hearing students speak a foreign language:

> I try to see Auslan as a language other than English, and I think it's recognized as such. I think students who are learning Mandarin don't come to the classroom and start talking to their teacher who can't—doesn't—speak a word in Mandarin. . . . You say, "Sorry, that's for your LOTE subject. When we're in this classroom, we use English as our means of communication."
>
> I can't see at this stage that we'd go past using it as a LOTE. We certainly don't intend using it as a means of communication in the foreseeable future . . . certainly for the length of this [school] charter, probably the length of my time as principal. . . . I cannot see any Auslan being used for anything else other than a LOTE at our school unless, of course, it became a directive of the Education Department, and I can't see that ever happening. (Participant 30)

This study exposes the educational positioning of Auslan in Victoria in the 1990s. Auslan was (and continues to be) excluded from oral education settings and marginalized in TC settings. The effect of this inclusion or exclusion of native sign language is to categorize Deaf students as either insiders or outsiders. In TC programs, Auslan and deaf adults may be given a marginal role; however, the hearing teachers maintain linguistic control. Adding Auslan to established approaches does little to bring about structural change; existing power structures remain intact, and Auslan is marginalized as merely an addition to the curriculum. The inclusion of minority students' first languages and community participation in school programs can shift attention away from the attitudes and approaches of educators whose actions empower or disable minority students (Cummins 1986). In this way, Deaf Studies and Auslan as a LOTE subject may have moved attention away from teachers' continued instruction in English. One can expect that adding the native sign language in this way will do little to improve the education of deaf students (Rodda, Cumming, and Fewer 1993). Only in bilingual programs are Deaf people and their language central to the educational system.

The dearth of research on deaf education by state authorities perpetuates the current practices. Educators and administrators with a deficit view of deaf students *expect* underachievement in education and remain unaware of deaf students' potential to succeed through the use of sign language. Hearing people maintain control of the structure and process of deaf education by defining language policy, curricula, and teacher education. Employing a small number of Deaf adults as LOTE instructors for just one or two hours a week will not threaten or disrupt the status quo. The structures in education protect the power of hearing professionals, who, by controlling the language used in the classroom, effectively include or exclude Deaf students. Denied connections to Deaf people and prevented from acquiring sign language, deaf children "lose access to a history of solutions created for them by other people like themselves" (Padden and Humphries 1988, 120).

Immersing deaf students in English-only environments with little or no access to the language and culture of the Deaf community puts them at considerable risk (for examples of the barriers to learning that schools erect, see Cambourne 1990). The situation of Deaf people in Australia parallels that of other minority groups whose language, culture, and identity are denied them by members of a dominant culture. Unlike other minority communities, however, deaf children are put further at risk by a lack of accessible linguistic input in school and at home. Deaf children who are born to hearing parents often fail to enter school with age-appropriate linguistic development. Their educational underachievement must be considered at least in part the result of disabling pedagogy:

> The handicap is that their hearing parents usually have a different ethnocultural identity which, lacking a shared language, they cannot pass on to their children. Moreover, they commonly do not advocate in the schools, community, courts, and so on for their Deaf child's primary language. Minority languages without parental and community support are normally endangered. The great advantage of the Deaf-World lies in the fact that there will always be intergenerational

continuity for sign language, for there will always be visual people
who take possession of that language in preference to any other and
with it the wisdom and values of generations of Deaf people before
them. (Lane 2007)

Incorporating Sign Language into Education: The Swedish Example

In Sweden, the acceptance of other languages, which is reflected in government policy, has enabled the country's Deaf community to argue for
recognition on a par with other minorities (Svartholm 1993, 291). The
acceptance of Swedish Sign Language and the positive view of deaf people
it engenders are some of the reasons for the success of bilingual programs
there (Svartholm 1994).

"The curriculum was followed by new syllabi, the same as those for
hearing pupils except for the language-specific subjects Swedish Sign
Language and Swedish as a second language for deaf students, and music
(which became "movement and drama" for the deaf). The curricula
goals, general as well as subject-specific, were consistent across all schools,
for deaf and hearing students" (ibid.).

The government used this report to draft a bill (Prop 1998/99) later
passed by the Swedish Parliament that accentuated the need for sign
language among deaf people, deaf-blind people, and some hard of hearing
children. The measure explicitly stated that the special schools for deaf and
hard of hearing children were obliged to "offer a sign language environment in which everyone as far as possible communicates in signs" (my
translation). The bill also stressed that such an environment could not be
provided by integrating into regular schools individuals or small groups
of deaf students who needed sign language. The special schools for deaf
and hard of hearing children remained the responsibility of the government in order to secure a sign language environment. Explicit reference
was made to the United Nations' *Standard Rules on the Equalization of Opportunities for Persons with Disabilities* (1993), which sets forth deaf students'
need for special schools and access to instruction in sign language.

Soon after 1996, work began again on revising the syllabi for schools
for deaf children. The group charged with this task deliberated on

whether to produce two different syllabi (one for deaf children, the other for hard of hearing children and children with CIs) and decided to create only one. The single syllabus would be written so that it gave the schools the opportunity and responsibility to meet every child's specific needs and qualifications. Henning, who actively participated in this work, pointed out that schools for deaf children must provide "a highly qualified sign language environment with the aim of bilingualism" but that each school may choose the teaching methods and goals for individual pupils.

In the guidelines for special schools, the two languages—Swedish Sign Language and Swedish—are now considered more or less in unity. An introductory section of the syllabus discusses the interdependence of these two languages for personal development, as well as for learning. Signing, speaking, reading, and writing are core areas; the pupils are given opportunities to use and develop their skills, as appropriate to their individual abilities.

In Sweden, children involved in the first research project in which deaf children from hearing families were brought into contact with deaf adults and deaf peers left school in 1991. Described as literate, confident bilinguals (Svartholm 1995), a study of forty subjects found that students with early access to Swedish Sign Language performed better on tests in Swedish (Heiling 1995). Svartholm reflected on the gains made in deaf education in Sweden:

> The bilingual model for teaching deaf children has clearly turned out to be successful. The outcome of it is a group of confident, literate young people—confident not only in their first language, Sign Language, but also in their second language, Swedish. To characterize them, the word "normal" is what first comes into my mind. There are virtually no differences between them and any other young people of the same age, except for the language they use. I hope that all other deaf children will be given the opportunity to grow up and be just as normal as these are. (1994, 61)

Language Policy in Australia

Educators and educational authorities who claim that parents have a choice of communication method in deaf education are spouting political rhetoric when the only language offered in the classroom is English. The international literature on deafness harshly criticizes educational practices that exclude or marginalize native sign languages and Deaf culture. If this is the case, a review of educators' actions is critical. In the case of the Deaf community, claims of diversity in communication methods have been empty and fail to address the general absence or marginalization of native sign languages.

Efforts to address issues of diversity must go beyond the instrumental to structures that control communication. The history of Deaf people in education also points to the importance of viewing communication within a social context. Doing so allows us to examine the power relationships that exist there. A critical concept of diversity and communication calls for educators to view the power relationships that structure and position the members of out-groups such as Deaf people. To avoid keeping oppression alive, we need to take a critical view of communication in action.

It is generally acknowledged that education is probably the most important issue for deaf people. In the view of Karen Lloyd (2001), past president of the Australian Association of the Deaf, it is also the most difficult issue on which to advocate and effect change. She is highly critical of the control that hearing people traditionally take:

> Generations of Deaf children have been and continue to be "educated" in a system controlled by people who are not deaf and who focus on deafness as a defect that needs to be "fixed." The system attempts to educate them using a language (English) that they do not know fluently and cannot fully access; a system that excludes Auslan, and if it uses signing at all insists on using a form of sign contrived by hearing people. And these generations of Deaf children have emerged with poor English skills, poor education, poor general knowledge, poor self-esteem and so on. . . . It is particularly revealing that we meet so many "experienced teachers of the deaf" who cannot communicate with us as deaf people. (ibid., 1–2)

Dominant Group Politics

In my view, the most significant barrier to a change in the language policy for deaf education is the dominance of teachers and administrators who are almost exclusively hearing and lack competence in the native sign language (for Australia, see Hyde, Power, and Cliffe 1992). With few Deaf teachers in many countries, the language that continues to dominate deaf education is the national spoken language. For example, a survey of Australian teachers of deaf children in 1998 identified only 8 out of 868 teachers who were culturally and linguistically Deaf; that is, less than 1 percent of the profession are deaf and have native skills or fluency in Auslan. In five states of Australia, deaf or hearing-impaired TODs numbered zero or one. With most teachers unable to adopt bilingual practices, there has been little acknowledgment that established practices conflict with bilingual theory or the movement in the Deaf community toward self-determination (Komesaroff 1998).

In 1992 Hyde, Power, and Cliffe reported virtually no use of Auslan by the 245 teachers of deaf students who responded to their survey. The few who claimed to be using it encoded the test sentences following the principles of Signed English. In a later study, more than half of the 188 teachers of deaf children who responded to a survey about their use of manual communication agreed with the following statement: Signed English is the most appropriate form of manual communication for educational purposes (Leigh 1995). With increased interest in Auslan and additional bilingual programs established since this survey, we can reasonably expect an increase in the number of teachers with Auslan skills to have occurred. However, most TODs continue to leave teacher education programs with little or no proficiency in Auslan. There is no requirement for Auslan fluency in most courses for TODs, no requirement for them to be fluent in Auslan when they enter training programs, and limited instruction during their training.

At the time of the survey, the greatest number of hours of Auslan instruction in courses qualifying TODs was 72 in Western Australia. In other states, Auslan instruction was minimal or nonexistent. Queensland provided 28 class hours in both Australasian Signed English and Auslan (D. Power, personal communication, July 8, 1997), and a university in Victoria provided 18 hours after a minimum of one semester of Signed English (R. Jeanes, personal communication, February 20, 1998). Another Victorian university and one in South Australia provided no instruction in either Auslan or Signed English. Australia compares badly with Denmark, which provides 510–580 hours of training in Danish

Sign Language for TODs, with a further 170 hours for teachers who are not yet competent in Danish Sign Language and want to teach it as a first language (Bergmann 1994).

An insufficient number of deaf teachers and a paucity of Auslan skills among TODs are the most significant barriers to providing bilingual education. The difficulty that hearing TODs face in acquiring a foreign language is an understandable disincentive to considering bilingual education. Acquiring a new language cannot be left until teachers reach the classroom. It may be too late to expect schools to provide professional development to ensure that TODs become fluent in Auslan and skilled in bilingual pedagogy. The level of professional development required for TODs may well be beyond the resources of many schools.

Given the extent to which language policy and practices for deaf children in Australian schools are controlled by predominantly hearing teachers, it is no coincidence that the language of instruction in most schools for deaf students is that of the dominant hearing and speaking community. Consequently, English remains the authoritative text in deaf education while Auslan is marginalized or excluded through the policies of TC and oral settings.

CHAPTER 3

Curriculum of the Hearing University

L EGAL REFORM IN THE 1990s led Australian universities to establish policies of equal opportunity and consider issues of diversity within their staff and student populations. Legislation such as the Disability Discrimination Act (Commonwealth of Australia 1992) sought to protect the rights of people with a disability, and the requirement for organizations to develop a Disability Action Plan was to detail the objectives and actions intended to increase these people's access to and participation in society. The principle of equity enacted in Australian university policy targets four categories of difference: women, indigenous peoples, people with disabilities, and people of non-English-speaking background. The measure of inclusivity of members of groups traditionally excluded from higher education is based on their increased participation and success (Nunan et al. 2000). A federal grant, the Higher Education Equity Program (HEEP), is available to Australian universities for projects whose purpose it is to improve the success of these students.

Deaf students are targeted in the university equity policy under the category "students with a disability." In 2001 I conducted a pilot study of deaf students enrolled in undergraduate teacher education programs to obtain information on their experiences in higher education. The study coincided with two larger HEEP-funded projects. The first one provided mentoring and a role model program for deaf university students and was followed by a second project in 2002 and 2003 that profiled the achievements of deaf adults qualified through higher education.

My study consisted of interviews with two deaf students (one in her second year, the other in her third year) at two different universities in Victoria. I knew one of the students well since I had been her instructor and tutor, advocated for her rights, supported her struggle for her children's access to Auslan, and encouraged her to enroll in a teacher education program. In conducting the study, I was highly aware of the way in which deaf students have been positioned in education and alert to issues of category politics. I was also sensitive to the way in which research and researchers have historically positioned deaf people as the subjects of research in much the same way as indigenous people have predominantly been researched (see Waitere-Ang and Johnston 1999). I decided to interview deaf students rather than hearing members of the faculty and university departments responsible for administering and providing services to deaf students in order to represent the voices that are overwhelmingly absent in the "hearing university."

I interviewed both participants in Auslan. I asked them to respond to a series of questions that focused on their motivation for becoming a teacher, issues of identity, and academic literacies (dealing with university studies in a second language). The interviews were videotaped and interpreted into spoken English for the purpose of transcription, and copies were provided to the participants. They were invited to make changes or additions to the transcripts, giving them an opportunity to expand on or correct what they had intended to say and to also check the accuracy of my transcription. Neither participant chose to make any additions or alterations to the transcripts. The interpretative framework used in the analysis of data in this study was "category" or "identity politics" and the construction of difference. As such, the framework determined what I noticed and registered as important (Held 1991, 15). It also played a significant part in my understanding of the way in which deaf people's identities are represented: "Who you are [seen to be] does matter" (Pettman 1992a, 131; cited in Bacchi 1996, 3).

The analysis of data focused on issues of "simple equality" and the positioning of deaf students by and within the "hearing university." The results are not intended to be representative of the experiences of deaf teacher education students generally. At the time of the study, these were the *only* deaf students undertaking undergraduate teaching degrees at their respective institutions. In this respect, they represented the total number of deaf students in their class and provided valuable insight into their experiences at an overwhelmingly hearing university. Furthermore, the study does not describe or compare university structures; rather, it is a descriptive and analytical account of the experiences of two deaf teacher education students who reflected on their progress in higher education.

The participants, referred to as Sally and Brooke, are both female, Australian born, prelingually and severely to profoundly deaf, and bilingual in Auslan and English. Both were raised as the only deaf child in their hearing families and educated in English. Sally attended oral schools for deaf children and communicated through speech and lipreading at home and at school. Brooke used Signed English at home and at school. Both of them acquired Auslan as teenagers through contact with the Deaf community or deaf friends and interpreters at school. Both have several close family members who are university graduates and work as teachers or in allied professions. During the study, one of the participants deferred her studies because of personal difficulties but has since returned to the university.

Sally attended my own university. We first met through the Deaf community and again when she participated in previous research I was conducting. When she enrolled at the university, I provided her with additional tutoring (interpreting sections of academic text into Auslan, explaining assessment requirements, and so on). Later I arranged for the university to provide a paid tutor to support her in her studies. I witnessed the difficulty she encountered accessing interpreters through the university and the effect it had on her first year of study. Brooke, whom I had not previously known, attended a different university; she was identified as a potential participant in the study through her profile in the Deaf community as one of a small number of deaf adults enrolled in a college.

Sally

When Sally arrived at the university, she learned that she would not be provided with interpreters for all of her classes. She was told there was insufficient funding, an inadequate number of interpreters to meet the university's requirements, and too little lead time to schedule interpreters by the time the faculty finalized their schedules (interpreters were sometimes sought only days before the beginning of classes; as a result, many times they had already accepted jobs at other institutions or were otherwise fully employed). This situation persisted throughout Sally's first year. She asked other students to take notes for her, borrowed their notes, and relied on lipreading during lectures, tutorials, and group discussions. Sally's later reflection on her first year at the university understates the ongoing frustration she expressed to me in e-mails, phone calls, and discussions at the time:

> First year was a bit difficult because I wasn't provided with interpreters or note takers full time. I had to rely on other students to take notes for me, but it was limited. I never received complete notes, so I really had to persevere and keep asking and asking and asking at Student Services, and finally it was organized, and I had interpreters and note takers. But the problem still came up when interpreters were sick or on vacation, and the problem is ongoing. . . . When I arrived and there weren't interpreters and there were no replacement interpreters or the note takers would come late, that was a big frustration for me.

During her first year at the university, Sally joined other deaf students in filing a complaint against the university under the Disability Discrimination Act of 1992 for its inability to provide them with full access to their courses. The case was heard by the Victorian Equal Opportunity Commission, which ruled in favor of the students. Sally was to be given access to an Auslan interpreter for all of her university classes and tutorials throughout her four-year program (Human Rights and Equal Opportunity Commission 2005b). The university was ordered to provide an adequate level of access through the provision of interpreters and note-takers.

This gave Sally physical access to her courses, but the lack of awareness of deaf students' needs on the part of the academic and administrative staff proved to be an ongoing barrier to her success:

> Most staff don't have awareness. . . . That's a problem when they're not aware of deaf people because here it is such a big place, and so few deaf people and students services don't tell instructors what deaf students need. I'd be interested to know if they receive any information about raising their awareness . . . to tell instructors that you have a deaf student in your class, and this is what they'll need because I always have to go and tell them "Hey! I'm deaf, and this is the interpreter," and they back off a little from that, and it should be done well before that.
>
> I think Student Services should promulgate something about deaf students' needs—to explain to instructors about interpreters' roles so that instructors understand that and don't get the wrong impression of what interpreters do.

It is no coincidence that Sally found the most support and got her best grades in a women's studies class. She felt that her experiences as a Deaf woman were both valued and valuable in a class that focused on minority politics and differences. She felt respected and affirmed by her tutor and peers and enjoyed the opportunity to raise hearing people's awareness of her identity. She told me she felt "the same as everyone else. . . . I found people respecting who I am, not that I'm deaf . . . but respecting *me*."

I asked Sally how she felt about entering a profession that was dominated by hearing teachers. She replied, "[I'm] wondering if some teachers will accept a deaf teacher, or will they back off from me? Some teachers have been good. I think it's possible for me to be assertive and for them to have to need to change their attitude. In the past I've had to change my attitude; I've had to use speech and do all the changes for them, so why can't they change for me now? I think that would be fair."

After completing her practice teaching at the school her deaf children attended, Sally reported that the teachers said "they're looking forward to me coming back to work there again. I drove home thinking . . . just because I'm . . . going to be a teacher. Why didn't they think that in the past? Why didn't they respect me when I was [just] a parent?"

Her comments are directed toward teachers of deaf children and the system of deaf education rather than toward university staff members and tertiary institutions. However, an incident at the university again raised the issue of identity politics and difference. Sally came to me one day, incensed that a tutor had crossed out the capital letter in the word "Deaf" and rewritten it as "deaf." She insisted that she had explained the meaning of this widely adopted convention among writers in the deafness field and had correctly used it to indicate cultural allegiance to the Deaf community rather than a member of the dominant "hearing" culture. She was hurt and angry and had erased the "correction," a symbolic act of defiance in which she resisted the identity that had been ascribed to her.

Brooke

Brooke, the second participant in the study, had a very different experience of university life—at least, initially. Provided with interpreters and note-takers for almost every lecture and tutorial, she focused her comments on her desire to be treated equally, even if this meant missing out on what she needed as a deaf student:

> The classes were good, and the tutors would treat me equally. They don't give me extra help, and sometimes if I ask for it, they'll say, "You need to go to the Learning Services area," and I think, oh well, they're treating me equally. Sometimes I might have a question about the essay and wonder if I've gone off the track because sometimes the English is a bit challenging, and I'll ask if they can read through my essay, and they say no, they'll answer my questions, but they won't read through my draft, and I asked my friends if they'd said the same thing to them, and they said yes. So I think that's good.

Having integrated easily into mainstream schools for primary and secondary education, she resisted being treated as different or positioned as
"deaf" rather than as an ordinary university student:

> The instructors and the tutors were good, but they knew me as a
> deaf person. They wouldn't know my name, but they remembered
> my face, and it was a bit embarrassing because sometimes—like at
> my old school, there were at least two or three other students who
> were deaf—but here I'm the only deaf student in the university
> studying education, so I kind of stand out, and I found that a bit
> embarrassing.
>
> Sometimes in tutorials when we're having group discussions I
> feel the instructors talk to the interpreters rather than to me. Some
> of them do that. Some of them are great; they understand and accept
> who I am, but some of them, like when we're filing out at the end
> of the class, they'll say "How are you?" and "Things going well?"
> but they'll say during the class, "Oh, could you please wait so I can
> talk to you?" . . . Sometimes like at roll call . . . they'll be going
> through the names, but they won't call out my name because they
> already know I'm here. I'd rather that they said my name so I could
> say "yes" through the interpreter.

Brooke's accounts of higher education illustrate the struggle she has experienced between her self-identity, as a member of a cultural and linguistic minority, and that imposed on her by the dominant group:

> I don't consider myself disabled, but I understand the meaning of the
> word "disability." I understand that . . . and I understand the com-
> munity's perception of that word, and I accept that I have a disability
> in hearing, but I'm not physically disabled. Sometimes they treat me
> as being deaf first—I was about to say "disabled," but no, I mean
> being deaf.
>
> I had problems with one instructor last year. I found that she
> would put me down in front of everyone if I would miss a class [or]
> because I was late. She'd say something like—when she was calling

the roll, in front of everyone that is—"Oh, you weren't here last week." And I know that she wouldn't say that to other students. And she'd say, "Oh, do you have a medical certificate?" And I'd come almost every other time, and I'd say to her, could we talk about this later, and she'd say no, and she'd continue talking, and I couldn't stand it. It was so embarrassing, and so sometimes they treat me as being deaf first.

Although she thought highly of a particular instructor, she gave examples of the way in which he focused on her difference and lacked understanding of how to treat a deaf student:

Every workshop, every lecture, he'd go to the interpreter and say, "Are you okay? Are you comfortable there? Are you standing in the right place? Do you want a break?" He was a lovely man, but it made me the focus of attention, and I didn't like that. Or if I didn't go to a workshop, in a lecture, in front of all the students, he'd ask me where I was, where I'd been. . . . He didn't understand deaf students, or he'd say to the interpreter, "Tell *her* to do this" or "Ask *her* . . ." so he didn't know how to be able to talk to me directly.

During the second interview with Brooke a year later, she told me she no longer had full access to interpreters. In fact, she was being provided with interpreters or note-takers for only two of her twenty-one hours of scheduled classes. She believed the reason was that she had missed a number of classes the previous semester and had been working overseas (at a school for deaf children) when a meeting was held to organize her support services. She said she was being "blamed" by the disability liaison officer at the university for her difficulties, which made her feel "rebellious, like I didn't want to be at university." She resorted to asking friends to take notes for her during classes, just as Sally had during her first year.

After Brooke's first year at the university, she sought meaningful ways of dealing with the university curriculum. She planned to teach deaf children and believed that her instructors did not understand how she could obtain a regular teaching degree. She gave examples of her continued efforts to seek modified assessment and school practicum requirements to further her understanding and experience of deaf education. For example, she asked to be placed at a school for deaf children for practice teaching: "They said no, I had to go to a regular school." Her request to be placed at a regular school with a deaf facility also met with disapproval:

> I wanted to go to a school where they had deaf students integrated, and they said no, I couldn't do that. I had to go to a fully hearing school because I'd already had my [practice teaching] at . . . [a deaf school], and I could do an integrated round in an integrated setting next year, but this year it had to be a hearing school. It was interesting because the first year I went to . . . [a primary school], and there were no deaf students there. It was fully hearing, but the teacher was really reluctant with me and didn't allow me to teach the whole class. I was just teaching small groups, like reading groups and that was all. She felt that someone in my situation couldn't teach the full class. But last year I felt very involved teaching at . . . [the deaf school], and I got . . . [the highest grade]. In the previous school I got . . . [a lower grade], so I know that if I go back to a hearing school, my grades will drop again. I want to build my confidence, too, and that's why I'd like to go back to a deaf school. . . . I have to go to a school where I don't know anyone, have no contacts, and I'll just have to do my best there. They're not seeing it from my perspective—being a deaf student, being isolated.

On another occasion, she asked for permission to focus on a deaf child's writing development for an assignment about the social theories of language: "They said no, I have to write it from a hearing [point of] view because I'm in a course studying regular education, so it's a bit disappointing." Persisting, she next attempted to negotiate the requirements for a sociology assignment and then for another assignment in language education:

> I'm studying sociology, and we had to interview a family about their educational background, and I asked if I could interview a deaf family, and they sort of said, oh well, uh, and I said, well, I'm going to

teach deaf children in the future. And so they said, oh, yes, okay. So I've had some wins.

[But] last year . . . I asked them if I could study a deaf child's reading, and they said no, and I said, well, what about a CODA [child of deaf adults]? I said, it's a *hearing* child of deaf parents, still a *hearing* child. And they said, that's okay, but I wasn't allowed to study a deaf reader. So it's interesting.

In our final interview Brooke had another language assignment due. She was to observe a literacy session and discuss it in terms of pedagogical theories. She asked whether she could observe a literacy lesson with deaf students and consider the extent to which the language theories she had been studying could be applied to deaf education: "They said, no, you have to do the assignment as it has been handed out, so that it's the same as all the other students' work. . . . I wanted to do it from a deaf point of view, to research that, and I thought it would be really exciting, but they said no, I had to do the same task as everybody else in the class."

Brooke was unsure how to teach deaf children using a bilingual approach. She knew of the increasing awareness and recognition of native sign languages, and as a deaf person fluent in Auslan, she intended to instruct in this language and teach English through reading and writing. She did not expect her university education to equip her with this information either in the mainstream teaching degree she was pursuing ("because they don't know about deafness") or in the class for teachers of deaf students offered at the same institution ("[because it] is focused on audiology and hearing"). She therefore sought her own ways of studying bilingual pedagogy and arranged to spend four months during the university break as a volunteer worker at a school for deaf children in the United States. Her university would not give her academic credit for this experience, however, and rejected her request to count the overseas work as part of her practice teaching requirement "because it is a special school." Brooke went anyway.

When she returned to Australia, Brooke spoke enthusiastically about everything she had experienced. Her work as a student teacher in a U.S. school for deaf students stood in stark contrast to her experiences in

Australian schools. The key point of difference for her was the large number of Deaf teachers in the United States:

> We don't have many deaf teachers [in Australia] for starters. I mean *Deaf* teachers of the deaf, so we can't really lobby for good support and maybe make our schools really strong. . . . In America they're really strong and, really, there's equal numbers of deaf and hearing teachers of the deaf. So I don't think we can compare. The principal was deaf also.

Brooke especially valued the feedback she received from deaf teachers:

> Deaf teachers are in the same situation as I am. We have something in common. The hearing teachers supported me, yes, but they didn't give me feedback really, not as much as the deaf teachers. Plus they [the deaf teachers] gave me positive feedback or they told me directly; they were honest with me—saying I was signing too fast or something like that. . . . It was because . . . [the deaf teachers] shared my culture.

Settling back into the "hearing university" now became significantly more difficult for Brooke. She felt more isolated than she had before her U.S. experience:

> When I came back to class, I thought, oh, it just doesn't seem to be relevant to me. There were excellent instructors, but, for instance, if they were talking about educating students, they'd say, "This is how you do it. Make sure that all the students are watching you because you have to be careful of this and this." And so it was great. It was from their experience, but they concentrate only on regular students, and so they're talking about having twenty or thirty students in a class, and I don't want to work in regular schools. I am going to work with the deaf, so I lost a lot of motivation when I came back, and I didn't attend many classes. . . . I wanted to start working now and not go to the university to learn how to do things in *their* classrooms.

Sally echoed Brooke's resistance to learning how to do things in *their* classrooms. She made a similar comment about the attitudes of hearing teachers of deaf students who had taught her children before she started work on her education degree. One day she exploded: "I had to do *their* degree to be respected!"

The universities represented in this study embrace a liberal view of inclusivity in which success is focused on the benefits to those who would not otherwise be involved in higher education. The goal of these programs is "simple equality," in which "everyone gets access to the same thing in the same form" (Rizvi and Lingard 1996, 22). Brooke rejoiced in her equal treatment by instructors even if it meant *not* getting what she needed as a deaf student. The unwillingness of her instructors to negotiate alternate assessment and practicing teaching requirements is a disappointing example of educators' resistance to the "broadening of curriculum choice and pedagogical practice" (ibid., 25). It is also a poignant example of how "conformity and obedience to rules . . . are based on the requirements of administrative convenience rather than moral principles" (ibid., 24).

A more critical concept of inclusivity is possible through "curricular justice" (Connell 1998, 94). This view of curriculum focuses on the relationships between students and teachers: "The problem is not so much in unequal shares of an educational service, as in the educational relationships embedded in that service which make its effects unequal or oppressive." Another term for this is the "politics of incorporation" (Bacchi and Eveline 1996, 79–80), in which women, for example, are added to "established institutional regimes without considering that these might need to change," or, as Foster (1992) described it, "adding *women* and not stirring." In much the same way, the deaf students in this study were accepted into universities with seemingly little or no attempt to consider or change the structures that serve to disempower and position them.

CHAPTER 4

Bilingual Education

Educational justice is complex, and requires attention not only to . . .
concerns of access and equity—but also to issues of the culture of schooling;
that is, the way things are named and represented, the manner in which
difference is treated and the ways in which the values, significations and
norms which govern life in schools are negotiated and established.

— *Rizvi and Lingard 1996, 25*

IN THE ANTITHESIS to curricular fundamentalism, bilingual educators
reject the "curriculum of the hearing"—a take on Ball's (1993) "curriculum of the dead"—and exploit, rather than ignore, the cultural capital
and linguistic resources that Deaf students and teachers bring to the classroom. The decision to instruct deaf children through speech, contrived
sign systems, native sign language, or (more recently) "sign-supported
speech" (the use of Auslan with English word order) continues to be a
highly contested issue among Australian educators. The high incidence
of childhood cochlear implantation has only served to fuel this debate.

It took quite some time before Australian educators accepted the
findings of research that recognized the linguistic legitimacy of American Sign Language (ASL) (Stokoe 1960) or suggested the importance of
instruction through native sign language (Cicourel and Boese 1972a,
1972b). At first they refused to generalize the results of these U.S. studies

to the Australian context, given the different origins of ASL and Australian sign language (MacDougall 1988). However, during the 1980s the recognition of native sign language was growing both nationally and internationally, and Australian educators were becoming aware of the movement that was challenging the approach traditionally taken in deaf education. In 1987 Auslan gained formal recognition as a community language and was included in the *National Policy on Languages* (Lo Bianco 1987). Two years later the first Auslan dictionary was published by Australian linguist Trevor Johnston (1989), and in 1991 the Deaf community was recognized as a cultural and linguistic minority in the government publication *Australia's Language: The Australian Language and Literacy Policy* (Department of Employment, Education, and Training [DEET] 1991). The DEET document described the use of Auslan for instruction in schools as controversial because most deaf children come from English-speaking families. In my view, the controversy arises more from the fact that most teachers of deaf children are English speakers.

Some educators responded enthusiastically to the calls for native sign language and Deaf culture to be positioned as central to the educational system. They were influenced by the emerging literature in the field (such as Lane 1984; Cummins 1984; Johnson, Liddell, and Erting 1989; Hansen 1990; Davies 1991a, 1991b; Grosjean 1992; Israelite, Hoffmeister, and Ewoldt 1992; Svartholm 1993; Ahlgren and Hyltenstam 1994; Mahshie 1995), visiting scholars, and visits to overseas bilingual programs such as those in Sweden and the United States. In 1987 the first bilingual pilot program was introduced in Tasmania, where a full-fledged program began running in 1991 (F. Gifford, personal communication, May 14, 1998). This was followed by two programs in New South Wales. By the end of the 1990s bilingual programs were operational in five of Australia's seven states or territories (although the intransigence of some educators and state systems would later become the basis of legal complaints by parents of deaf children; see chapter 5).

The first bilingual programs in Australia adopted the principles common to most international bilingual programs for deaf students at the time (see North 1993; Gifford 1997; Paterson and O'Reilly 1997). A large body of research and commentary supported the use of native sign language, and the Ontario Ministry of Education had commissioned a comprehensive literature review of the effects of native sign language on majority language acquisition (Israelite, Ewoldt, and Hoffmeister 1992). Israelite et al. identified four characteristics of bilingual programs for Deaf children:

- Native sign language is used as the first language and the language of instruction.
- The majority language is introduced when students begin to acquire native sign language.
- Deaf culture and Deaf role models are an important part of the educational program.
- Parents are introduced to the culture and community of Deaf people and supported in their learning of the native sign language.

The introduction of bilingual programs in Australia was largely attributable to the efforts of small groups of teachers, parents, and Deaf people. The initial project in Tasmania arose because those involved realized that deaf students' educational and cultural rights could not be fully attained without a "significant philosophical shift" (Gifford 1996, 2). The teachers "relinquished ownership" of the deaf students and recognized that "being treated equally does not imply that deaf and hearing students should receive the same treatment, when they clearly have different needs" (ibid., 8). In New South Wales, parents and members of the Deaf community turned to a private institution, the Royal New South Wales Institute for Deaf and Blind Children, after unsuccessfully lobbying the state educational authority for a bilingual program. A private bilingual preschool (the Roberta Reid Centre) and a private bilingual primary school (the Thomas Pattison School) opened in 1992 and 1993, respectively. In other states, teachers and members of the Deaf community had been lobbying for change since the early to mid-1990s (see Iskov 1994; Richards 1997), and bilingual programs were established in Western Australia, South Australia, and Victoria.

However, most education administrators, teacher certification authorities, and universities that train teachers of deaf students infrequently acknowledge the need for teachers to be proficient in Auslan and well versed in bilingual pedagogy. Growth in the number of programs has preceded access to professional development and has not been accompanied by changes in teacher certification requirements. Frustrated by the unwillingness of some education officials to introduce bilingual programs, the parents of deaf students in several states have filed complaints under the Disability Discrimination Act of 1992 (see chapter 5). A belief that was (and may still be) prevalent among educators and policy makers at the time was that disagreement over the use of speech, contrived sign systems, or Auslan was merely a *communication* issue and a pedagogical debate among teachers. However, this conviction ignores the fact that it is an issue of *language* rather than *communication* mode.

My research into language practices in deaf education in the mid-1990s identified the general paucity of Auslan skills and knowledge of bilingual pedagogy among teachers of deaf children. Universities that trained these teachers provided minimal or no instruction in Auslan or bilingual approaches, thereby making it difficult for schools to consider pedagogical change. For example, the only Victorian university training for teachers of deaf children (one of only four institutions in the whole of Australia) included a *four-hour* introduction to the language and culture of the Deaf community in its one-year postgraduate course. By 1998 it had increased instruction in Auslan to 18 hours, and in 2001 teachers were required to complete a Level 1 Auslan course (provided by another institution) for a total of 36 hours. This compares very poorly with countries such as Denmark, which provides its teachers with more than 500 hours of instruction in Danish Sign Language (Bergmann 1994). In Sweden, teachers of deaf children are now required to *enter* their training with a certain level of proficiency in Swedish Sign Language.

While there is anecdotal evidence that increasing numbers of Australian teachers of deaf children studied Auslan in the 1990s, inadequate levels of Auslan instruction in teacher training programs have limited opportunities for in-service training. The absence of a requirement for Auslan fluency for employment or certification purposes has perpetuated the dominance of English in deaf education. The barriers to change have been both personal and structural. Many teachers appeared resistant to a change in policy that would require them to instruct in a language in which they had limited or no skill.

In the late 1990s, when I surveyed all of the educational settings for deaf students and contacted centers for itinerant teachers of deaf children in every region and state, I found that less than 3 percent of the 868 teachers who were working in deaf education were themselves Deaf or hard of hearing (Komesaroff 1998). Teachers who could be considered culturally and linguistically Deaf (that is, deaf and fluent or native users of Auslan) numbered only eight—less than 1 percent of the profession.

Supporters of bilingual education, however, have centered their investigations on power relations in deaf education, the positioning of Deaf people and their language, and issues of exclusivity. They have taken into account the language, culture, and minority status of Deaf students, thus viewing them as "minority language bilinguals" (Grosjean 1996). In doing so, they have concluded that the general academic failure and underachievement of Deaf students is the result of "educational disabling" (Cummins 1989)—not students who have a "disability." With the growing recognition of the legitimacy of native sign languages, researchers have begun to explain the failure of contrived sign systems (such as Signed English) on the basis that they are not languages at all. Rather, they have described these systems as follows:

- artificial codes that lack both the features of natural languages and the social context within which natural languages exist
- methods that are used only in a school context, usually for interaction with teachers, but not by communities for "real purposes" (Erting 1992)
- awkward and confusing techniques that violate the linguistic structure and morphological rules of native sign languages (see Bouvet 1990; Reagan 1995)
- incomplete and ineffectual models of language that delete a considerable amount of linguistic information (see Mayer and Lowenbraun 1990; Drasgow 1993; Leigh 1995)

The World Federation of the Deaf (WFD) and the Australian Association of the Deaf (AAD) have also called for changes in deaf education. The WFD's Scientific Commission on Sign Language (WFD 1993, 12) recommended that "teachers of the deaf must be expected to learn and use the accepted natural sign language as the primary language of instruction." The AAD's policy on education called for the following:

1. the right of Deaf children to have full early exposure to sign language and to be educated as bilinguals or multilinguals with regard to reading and writing.
2. the recognition of Auslan, the sign language of the Australian Deaf Community as the first language of a Deaf child, which will ensure that Deaf children acquire their first language with full fluency. The right of Deaf children to be educated bilingually with:
   • the national sign language as the main language of instruction for academic subjects the [*sic*] instruction in the national spoken and written language should occur separately but in parallel as is usual for other bilingual educational programs for other languages.
3. the [*sic*] instruction of English occurs best in the written form. In order to teach and explain how to use and understand English, Auslan should be used as a teaching language. Deaf children should choose whether to learn the spoken form.
4. the provision of sign language instruction for parents and professionals working with Deaf children.
5. teachers of Deaf children to learn and use Auslan as the primary language of instruction. (Australian Association of the Deaf 2003, http://jdsde.oxfordjournals.org/cgi/reprint/9/2/210.pdf; accessed June 3, 2007)

One School's Journey

The case study described in this chapter is a powerful example of how a school community can alter its language policy and practices to foster deaf education. The study documents the process of change and collaboration among teachers, parents, and researcher as the group considered introducing Auslan and adopting a bilingual pedagogy. The reconsideration of the existing language policy at Apple Hills (as it is referred to here) was propelled by the teachers' dissatisfaction with the deaf students' academic achievement and their own practices. A key finding of this study is that, in making a transition to a bilingual approach, it is essential to garner the support of the students' parents.

Changing teaching practices can be a slow and difficult process (Cohen, McLaughlin, and Talbert 1993), and resistance will likely be encountered if the teachers lack support or are required to make significant changes (Johnson 1993). An opportunity for me to work with the school community came with the facility coordinator's positive response to my invitation (sent to all of the possible research sites in Victoria) to take part in a study of language practices in deaf education (see chapter 2 for a description of the research). Unlike the other two case study schools, this community saw the project as a chance to learn about Auslan and bilingual pedagogy. The collaborative nature of my work with this school is best described as an "educative" research paradigm (Gitlin, Siegel, and Boru 1993).

I responded to the teachers' and parents' requests for information and took an active role in the school's transition to bilingual education. As such, I was "clearly positioned (passionate) within the domain of a political question or stance" (Fine 1994, 23) and was "openly political" (Gitlin et al. 1993, 204) when discussing alternatives to teachers' practices and challenging the prevailing approach to deaf education. The members of the school community believed that this research would provide them with knowledge and support that would otherwise be difficult to obtain due to their isolation from the state's capital city. They wanted a clear understanding of how a bilingual program might operate in their setting; the nature of their inquiry therefore placed me at the center of educational change. I was eager to discover what had led them to consider Auslan and what issues had supported or blocked change to language policy and practice. The outcome of the research is an example of the sort of community change that is possible in educational research.

I visited Apple Hills every two weeks throughout the school year. Because the school is several hours away from a capital city, I remained there for two to three days at a time and stayed in the housing provided for deaf students who came from outside the local area. I had access to students, teachers, and parents outside regular school hours, and this enabled me to build relationships with members of the school community. I had a unique opportunity to observe and document the way in which a group of teachers and parents questioned (and ultimately rejected) the use of Signed English and a Total Communication language policy. I was able to explore teachers' beliefs about language use with deaf students and discuss with them the implications for change.

The facility coordinator believed that this study provided an impetus for the school to develop a bilingual program, and the teachers connected my involvement in the school to the changes that ultimately occurred there. I was aware, however, that "it is not the outsider that brings about improvement and change in teachers and schools—it is the school that improves itself. The staff of the school hold the key; if they decide to change themselves then things begin to change" (Murdoch and Johnson, 1994, 30). Indeed, if projects are conceived from the outside the community, the role of an outsider can be problematic (ibid.). The teachers in this school community stood out from other professionals in the field as being open to change, their willingness fuelled by their dissatisfaction with the status quo.

The staff of this deaf facility worked at three school sites in the district: a primary school for students in kindergarten to grade 6 (five- to eleven-year-olds), a secondary school for grades 7 to 10 (twelve- to fifteen-year-olds), and a senior-secondary school for grades 11 and 12 (sixteen- to eighteen-year-olds). Teachers supported twenty-four deaf students in withdrawal sessions and regular classes. They provided small-group teaching and individual tutoring; some of the staff members offered interpreting services—a Signed English interpreter worked at the primary school, and two of the TODs, who had Auslan skills, interpreted for students in grades 11 and 12. When the study began, most of the teachers communicated with the deaf students through the simultaneous use of spoken and Signed English, and the facility endorsed a policy of Total Communication.

All seven teachers of the deaf students, eight parents, and the regional manager of the Department of Education participated in the study. All were hearing and most were female. The teachers' experience in deaf education ranged from five months to almost thirty years, and more than half of the teachers had obtained TOD qualification within the previous decade. In terms of language skills, five of the seven teachers used Signed English, usually simultaneously with spoken English (two of these teachers also used some Auslan signs and fingerspelling but followed English word order). Two teachers were using Auslan: One was a paraprofessional interpreter, and the other was studying Auslan part-time. Two other teachers had received some instruction in Auslan during their TOD training but considered it inadequate to acquire fluency. The teachers had received no pre- or in-service training in bilingual methods.

Data collected included interview transcripts, field notes of classroom participation, and observation notes. Most of the teachers were interviewed three times during the study (one teacher who went on leave, as well as her replacement, were present for two interviews), the second and third interviews drawing on my interpretation of the emerging data. Two formal group meetings were held with the parents, and several informal chats took place with individuals or small groups of parents. All of the interviews and formal meetings were taped, and transcripts were provided to the participants, who were invited to make additions or changes. Interviews were semistructured and became free-flowing discussions about issues and practices in deaf education. In the thirty-five classes I attended, I adopted a participant-observer role: I sometimes modeled bilingual practices, tutored or interpreted for the students, or presented demonstration lessons. This enabled teachers and parents to observe my use of Auslan with *their* children in *their* classrooms. This latter technique appeared to be effective since most of the teachers and parents had incorrectly assumed their children would not understand Auslan because they lacked previous contact with it.

Teachers' Beliefs

When this project began, the teachers were aware of the growing interest in native sign languages in the field of deaf education, as well as the introduction of Auslan into a number of schools in Australia. Four teachers (including the two who already had some Auslan skills) believed it was important for deaf children to develop skills in Auslan as a strong first language, a foundation on which other learning could be built. The remaining three teachers were unsure of the benefits of Auslan and were concerned that it would impact negatively on students' acquisition of spoken and written English. Some of the teachers assumed Auslan would be *foreign* to their students and unnecessary for those who communicated orally. Others questioned how literacy levels could be improved if English were taught as a second language through native sign language. Their main concerns in considering a bilingual program were the place of speech, the method of introducing new practices, financial support for a new program, uncertainty about how a new program could be established in their setting, and the approach to take with parents. They assumed the main stumbling block would be the absence of the simultaneous use of spoken English, something the parents expected.

Several teachers already believed that Signed English was inadequate and inappropriate for instruction, particularly with older students. In grades 11 and 12, the TODs interpreted for the students when they faced sophisticated language produced at a rapid rate. They had already adopted Auslan in response to the request from previous students who had complained that Signed English was inadequate. Those working above junior primary level believed they had little hope of accurately producing manually coded English, and all of the teachers appeared to accept the need for change. The feeling among the group is best summed up by one teacher's comment: "We can't just continue doing something that is not working" (34).

Working with three different age groups, these teachers had more opportunity than most to see their students' longer-term educational outcomes. Most of them agreed that the gap had widened between deaf and hearing students by midprimary school. By this stage, the language used in the classroom was "more detailed," increasingly complex, and "less concrete." The teachers noticed that some of the students failed to understand the instructions or explanations they gave in Signed English, and they were forced to repeat or rephrase the information. By the final years of school, the teachers felt unable to compensate for the students' lack of first-language skills: "We're trying to feed language in now; it's too late. The expected level is just far above what we can give them. I'm spending my time modifying textbooks, modifying work sheets, modifying everything to bring it down to their level. . . . I think the problem is the kids I see now haven't really got a great first language, and that is such a difficulty trying to get to a second language when you've got a problem first language. There are so many gaps. . . . I'm struggling even to help them because I have to go back to basics so often and start again" (12).

Another factor that raised the teachers' awareness of deaf students' unsatisfactory progress was the contrast they saw between the deaf students and their hearing peers. The teachers met regularly to discuss the students' development. When the teachers at the secondary or senior-secondary school described the inadequate language and literacy skills, poor engagement, and behavioral difficulties of some of the students, the teachers in the primary school reflected on the approach they themselves were taking with students with similar levels of hearing loss:

> What I am dealing with now [at the postprimary level] makes us reflect on six years ago. . . . We can look at kids now . . . in grade 4 and say, "That is exactly where these guys were when they were in grade 4." So should we continue along with what we are doing? Are we being successful? . . . In a way, the reason I have gone to Auslan is because I think what we have done has fallen down, and it has achieved with kids who have a bit more hearing, but that's not what we're on about. We're trying to teach kids who are deaf, not kids who have got a bit more hearing. (10)

The dissatisfaction of some of the teachers with the school's language policy was also fuelled by their contact with deaf adults. In the past, they had taught deaf children from deaf families and were aware of the language advantage those children had over youngsters from hearing families. Some of the teachers had also worked or studied with deaf peers. One of these teachers had worked for many years in another school with a Deaf colleague who had been educated at Gallaudet University (the only liberal arts university for deaf and hard of hearing students, located in Washington, D.C.) and was well respected in the Melbourne community. Those teachers who lacked Auslan skills felt frustrated that they had little alternative to using Signed English, despite their diminishing confidence in its efficacy. One teacher commented, "I've probably always thought in the background that there is a need for something else, but I haven't had any . . . contact with Auslan. So it was just out there, you know; it was another option that I didn't really understand or know about. But in my own thoughts, the more I could move myself into a kind of pidgin, the more I was moving, I guess unknowingly, moving towards Auslan" (10).

Another teacher, who had been trained in the late 1980s, was angry that she had become aware of the controversy over language practices in deaf education only when she was seen referring to a Signed English dictionary during a field placement at a school for deaf children (which has since adopted a bilingual approach):

> That's what I was taught, so I didn't know anything different! . . .
> Auslan never, ever got a mention [in my course] until that first time
> I walked into . . . [the school] and that woman nearly tore me to
> shreds because I had a yellow book or a green [Signed English]
> book. . . . I mean, there was a little inkling [at the university], but it
> was still hidden; it wasn't talked about! . . . I never, ever really had a
> belief that Signed English was "it" and that's the way we go; it was
> just an acceptance that that's what you did. . . . I had always thought
> that Signed English is really deficient in lots and lots of areas and
> made access to language for deaf kids really limiting. . . . I always
> thought there's got to be something better than Signed English but
> never had much contact with Auslan itself. (14)

Over the course of the research project, this teacher became convinced of the advantages of Auslan for deaf children: "If Auslan does produce better results in teaching kids English, then they have got a right to that; so I am happy to give it a go" (14). She and her colleagues recognized the deficiencies of Signed English, but without Auslan skills they had little alternative but to continue instructing in English. They also faced the difficulty of acquiring Auslan as an in-service teacher and continuing to use the language skills they knew were inadequate:

> Annoyance and, yes, I suppose [I feel] anger because, you know, for
> a while there I suppose you blame yourself. You are doing the wrong
> [thing] by the kids, and it is my fault, and I should have known better,

but then again I think really it was up to them. They should be giving us everything; this is what is available to the deaf and doing it like that rather than just telling us about Signed English and that was it! I mean that was unfair to the Deaf community and unfair to us. If they want us to educate deaf, deaf children, then we really need to know what deaf people feel and that "other language" that existed. (14)

I feel as if a lot of my beliefs have been challenged, but they have been for some time, so it is not so drastic or sudden. . . . And I suppose the thing that I feel along with the other staff is an "uncomfortableness." Well, I can't give this, I can't deliver this. You are supposed to be a professional, educating these deaf kids, and yet here is this whole wall that is saying there is another way, and you are thinking, well, I can't do this; I haven't got the skills; I haven't got the knowledge, and that is an uncomfortable or maybe threatening feeling (9).

I think my level of knowledge of Auslan is very low. . . . I believe in it, and I believe the concept of it being a deaf first language, and the kids need to have a first language before they can progress to another language, but my knowledge is really limited, and I find that perhaps a bit of a frustration. (10)

The last teacher (10) quoted was perhaps the most apprehensive of his colleagues about the impact of a transition to a bilingual program. He asked how training would be provided, how teachers could receive sufficient support to enable them to acquire a new language, whether he would be able to learn Auslan, and how long it would take to do so. How could he teach while using a language he was just beginning to learn? He viewed time release—away from the pressures of the classroom—as essential to his learning Auslan. His frustration was heightened by his belief in the importance of Auslan to his students.

Another teacher was similarly filled with self-doubt: "Am I good enough? Am I capable of getting information across? I mean, if I'm not, I'm delaying their education; I'm delaying their learning and gaining of knowledge, and you can't afford to do that" (17). Yet another teacher said, "When I modeled bilingual techniques, the teachers began to see how effective they could be. I just saw you work today, and I was really very impressed . . . because I was going to present that lesson to those three kids myself . . . and I know that I would have trouble with the language, just going through the explanation of some of the terms and the concepts. . . . But it was obvious that they understood it" (9). Still another teacher commented, "A good enough argument why you should change, seeing the kids using it. I mean you'd have to be blind Freddy not to see the differences that day, those two days, when you were working with them and we were watching. They did understand, and they got it like that! They got it really quickly; whereas Signed English, we would have still been trying to explain it to them" (14).

As the teachers' beliefs about language practices changed, some began to move away from the strict coding of Signed English to the use of signs they considered to be more "visually meaningful." Two teachers tried to use Auslan signs but felt hampered by their inadequate understanding of the structure of the language and by the difficulty in moving away from English. Despite this, one of these teachers noticed that his students understood him more easily when he attempted to convey the underlying meaning of a spoken or written utterance rather than coding it strictly into Signed English: "I know there is a change happening, but I don't understand it . . . a change in the kids and their understanding" (10). He concluded that Auslan should become the language of instruction at the school but clearly sought the parents' support: "If I knew Auslan I would use it. . . . What I would do, I would do the exact opposite of what I do now. What I do now is I use Signed English and try to butcher it basically so the kids can understand it. So I will take it, simplify it down, and I will use different word order, like the idea of establishing context and then explaining, so that is where I've moved before. But I think in a way, if it was my decision without worrying about what parents' beliefs were, I'd rather be in Auslan and then moving them toward English. . . . I'm not prepared to jump off on this if we don't get support, and I guess that is the same for everyone: parents and teachers. There is no point in someone tearing off to do Auslan if we are not going to move that way in what I would see as a coherent manner" (10).

Gaining Parent Support

From the start of this study, the teachers at Apple Hills recognized the necessity of gaining parental support, and this became a critical issue.

They said the parents wanted their children to have a "normal" education and live in the hearing world; the teachers expected the parents to
be uncomfortable with Auslan, particularly those who communicated
orally with their children. Consistent with the view of other professionals I have interviewed in relation to deaf education, these teachers believed that the parents were in a position of power and would have the
final say over language policy at the school. Some of them made comments such as "It is no use, I suppose, fighting with parents over communication" (14), and "You've got to be careful how you deal with them
because they are the real crucial part—they are *their* kids, *their* decision,
their choice" (12). The teachers expected the parents to resist Auslan due
to fear of losing their children to the Deaf community and relinquishing
control of the school program (which Deaf people could come to
dominate).

The teachers also believed that the parents would be afraid that their
children might lose any oral language skills they had developed. The
coordinator explained that "if they [the parents] see Auslan as a Deaf
culture language and they are excluded from it, even by their own
choice, then they see that as a loss" (9). The degree of support for Auslan
was expected to depend on the degree to which the parents accepted
and understood their child's deafness: "Some of them don't see their
children as Auslan users or . . . [as] leaving them and going into this Deaf
world or anything. They don't want to visualize that. Some of them are
still coming to terms with the fact that the kids are deaf" (9).

The facility coordinator had a more positive view of the parents. He
recognized their need for information in order to make an informed
choice, just as he and other teachers had done. He did not believe their
current beliefs would be a barrier to change. He asked me to introduce
and explain the nature of Auslan and bilingual pedagogy to the parents.
He and the other teachers believed that I was in the best position to talk
to the parents not only because of my knowledge of Auslan and bilingual
education but also because I was an outsider to the community.

The parent support group (PSG) at Apple Hills included parents of
the deaf children in the facility, the facility coordinator, and other TODs.
At the first meeting I attended, I explained the purpose of my research.
The next day the PSG president asked me to meet again with the parents,

only this time without the teachers. When I discussed this invitation with the coordinator, he and the other teachers agreed that the parents needed an opportunity to freely question the school's language policy. Parents were encouraged to attend, particularly those who had already expressed concern about changes in the language policy. The facility coordinator supported the need for change and remained optimistic that, with the backing of most of the parents, the school would introduce a bilingual program. He stressed the importance of allowing teachers and parents to make up their own minds without feeling pressured and of respecting the rights of everyone in the school community. He anticipated opposition from some parents but did not believe it would be insurmountable:

> We've got a problem. We recognize that Signed English doesn't answer that. We've also got a problem, we know that the literacy skills of our kids are low. Now I think for a long time most of us felt, well, that's deaf kids; that's life.
>
> I think we really have to take it a step at a time. I think we as a staff have to look at how we can get knowledge, get training, and work it that way and get parents' support to begin a program with the children just at what level or whatever I don't have enough understanding at the moment to do that. (9)

The second formal meeting I had with the PSG, this time without the teachers present, went as the teachers expected. The parents' major concern was the effect Auslan might have on their children's development of spoken language and acquisition of literacy. They had been advised by teachers in the past to use speech in preference to sign language and to use Signed English if oral communication failed. Not having been told about Auslan (and thinking it must be a new method of communication), they had assumed that Signed English was the language of the Deaf community. Some of them had expected that Auslan could be used simultaneously with spoken English; others said they thought it was a "code for English" or "English without the small words." Most assumed it would be foreign to their children or was simply not needed because their children were "oral." The parents whose children communicated orally expected them to become frustrated in the absence of speech and feared that Auslan would harm their existing oral skills or prevent further speech development. They also worried that Auslan would reduce the social interaction between the deaf and hearing children at the school, although this was already minimal.

The parent who was employed as a Signed English interpreter pointed out that at that time only limited communication took place between the deaf and the hearing students despite their use of Signed English. The other parents respected her views, as she was a highly proficient signer (in Signed English) and was considered to have provided the most consistent model of Signed English to her child at home. They had expected her response to Auslan to be cautious because of the possible threat to her employment if the school adopted a bilingual policy. However, she explained to the other parents: "I'm looking at it as a parent. . . . Patrick is fourteen, and his English is lucky to be grade 4. . . . Well, it's failed. Something has failed him, and we've signed since Patrick was two!" (39).

This parent had observed a demonstration lesson I had conducted with the deaf primary-aged students and subsequently became convinced of the advantage of Auslan over Signed English. This was the first critical incident (that I observed) that clearly changed a parent's views. During morning assembly one day, I witnessed a child's misunderstanding of an announcement about school rules that resulted from the interpreter's literal translation of the message into Signed English. The vice principal was reinforcing the school rules by reminding the children that certain things were not allowed, including fighting, kicking, and swearing. Word for word the interpreter signed WHAT-YOU-DO-IN-YOUR-OWN-HOMES-IS-UP-TO-YOU-BUT-THERE-WILL-BE-NO-SWEARING-AT-SCHOOL. The speaker's inflection was not communicated, so his meaning was misinterpreted. One deaf child nudged his friend and signed excitedly: SHE-SAID-WE-CAN-SWEAR-AT-HOME! I discussed what I had seen with one of the teachers, and we agreed that I should have an impromptu discussion with the children about the morning's announcement.

Sitting in a detention room with six deaf students and observed by two of their teachers and one parent, I asked the children about the school rules and what the vice principal had said at assembly. The child

I had observed maintained that the teacher had said they could swear at home; one child fervently disagreed; and the others were unsure. I explained what the speaker had meant, using Auslan signs such as PROHIB-ITED and UP-TO-YOU! and RISKY with regard to what they might do at home (with an expression of "woe betide you if your parents catch you!"). The children understood my signing, and I could see them mimicking and incorporating some of the key signs into their own conversations (signs for "kicking," "swearing," "bullying," and so on). One sign stumped them, though, and this was the sign for "deliberate." When I realized they did not understand it, I role-played the meaning of "deliberate" and "by accident." As a way of modeling the connection between Auslan and literacy, I wrote the English words for the interesting concepts or key signs we had used, while the children signed them back to me when I had finished the list. They had not only acquired new Auslan signs but were also able to read the English translations. The parent who observed the lesson explained to other parents at the PSG what it had been like:

> "This is what you really have to see. . . . I went to the meeting the other night and asked all these questions, how does it [Auslan] work; I mean I just didn't understand. The next morning I went into the classroom, and I watched how you worked with them, and I was amazed. I was really amazed. . . . The word 'deliberate' for a start. We've never used the word 'deliberate' at home! Patrick is nearly fourteen; he doesn't know what the word is; it's never really come up. . . . And it just came across to me that, having a fourteen-year-old and working at school, that I had never used the word 'deliberate.' . . . That's right; he would not know how to read the word 'deliberate.'" (39)

This discussion prompted the parents to ask for a demonstration of Auslan. Some had not seen it before and did not understand how it differed from Signed English. I signed some stories in Auslan using children's books so the parents could follow. One parent commented on a sign (a grammatical marker) that was repeated throughout the story. After this introduction some of the parents began to recognize the nativelike structure of their children's signing despite their lack of exposure to Auslan. For instance, one parent said, "It's not I'M-GOING-TO-GO-AROUND-TO-THE-SHOP-ON-THE-BIKE or something like that. Anyway, it's BIKE SHOP GET MONEY" (40). This struck a chord with another parent: "He must have decided that 'I want an apple,' and all that came out of his mouth was APPLE-PEELED-MUM. And I looked at him because he's thought 'I want a peeled apple,' and it's APPLE-PEELED-MUM! And I looked at him with a stunned look because it must have been after the meeting—because immediately I thought 'You've Auslan-ed [*sic*] that!' " (42).

It was clear in my discussions with the parents that they had expected Signed English to lead to their children's academic success and literacy. At the same time, hearing professionals had convinced them that deaf children would necessarily be language delayed and could not be expected to achieve the level that hearing children attained. The meeting ended as the parents expressed their concern over the inadequacy of Signed English and their children's unsatisfactory English language development.

The next meeting began with their expressions of anger about the guidance given to them by medical staff and teachers when they had first discovered their child's deafness. They related the counsel they had received, which encouraged them to view deafness as a disability and warned them that sign language would interfere with their child's spoken language development: "You were told, 'Don't go down that road [sign language], or they'll never, ever talk, and how are they going to live in a hearing world?' " (42).

In addition, they were highly critical of the parent advisers who, in their view, had handled the issue of communication incorrectly and given them the wrong advice. Several parents expressed support for Auslan; some had been influenced by their child's positive response to it, and others had simply recognized the inadequacy of Signed English and their child's poor educational achievements. Another couple recounted a second critical incident. Their son was an avid athlete, but his parents had told me that he felt isolated and frustrated with his hearing teammates. He was unable to understand the coach and embarrassed when his father attempted to interpret for him. I told his parents of an upcoming sports event in the Deaf community and suggested they take him.

In contrast to his usual reticence when meeting strangers, he inter-acted immediately and comfortably with a large group of Deaf people he had just met—to his parents' amazement. Unlike their son, they were filled with fear and felt a lack of belonging as they stood among the Deaf community and understood, for the first time, how their son had always felt as the only deaf child in a hearing family and a hearing world:

> I will never, ever forget that experience as long as I live. . . . I hated doing it, but it just reversed the roles. . . . He had never been ex-posed to it [Auslan] before, and all I can say is this—that after having that experience, there is no doubt that if you put them in a situation to try and teach them something, that's the way to go. You have to worry about your oral [skills] after that. So I think it's important that they get that first, the Auslan. . . . He understood everything that was going on in amongst fifteen people on a field that he's never laid eyes on. It was unbelievable; I wished I'd had a video.
>
> How long was he there the other day? Ten minutes! Wouldn't have been ten minutes, and there's fifteen people that he's never met before, and he's yakkin' away like you'd never believe. And that's not him; he's not like that. Now why did he do that there, and yet he won't do it here? He's comfortable; it's gotta be. It was an unbe-lievable experience. . . . I don't mind admitting it, I feel a little bit sad for the fact that we had to have that experience to realize that he was that happy there. (41)

As a result of their experience, both parents vigorously supported the introduction of a bilingual program at the school. By halfway through the study, it was clear that several other parents had also changed their convictions. The parent group was now putting pressure on the teachers to introduce a bilingual program. Although not yet all of the parents endorsed a change in the language policy, many of them were eager for the transition. The facility coordinator explained: "Some of the par-ents—actually they're screaming at us, 'Come on! Get into it!' So we've sort of got a real cross-section now of a group over here that's really strong, the bulk in the middle, and a few there that are very frightened and hesitant and want nothing to do with it. And that's probably how it should be; we'd be worried if they were all one way or the other" (9).

Although the parents who supported Auslan wanted to see it introduced as soon as possible, they were realistic about the time required to establish a bilingual program. They understood that staff members would need to acquire a new language and that doing so takes time and support. However, a sense of urgency pervaded their requests for a bilingual program. Some were convinced that their child's lack of progress was the result of inadequate language practices and that any further delay would prove costly in terms of lost opportunities for language development: "As much as you might want it tomorrow, you're not going to have five qualified, very able Auslan people in the classroom tomorrow morning. We can maybe use a bit of parent power if we decide to push that process along, and I think that's justified" (47).

Around this time some of the teachers began to doubt that a bilingual program could be set up at the school. They pointed to their coworkers' lack of Auslan skills. One teacher questioned his colleagues' commitment to Auslan and their ability to implement a bilingual program. He wondered whether it was right to expect teachers to learn Auslan and how likely it was that a Deaf adult could be convinced to work in the area given its relative isolation from a large city. He said these problems could not be solved quickly. This teacher's concerns clearly had a negative effect on the other teachers' morale. Several began to wonder whether a bilingual program could succeed and whether its implementation would be delayed or even abandoned. A teacher (with strong Auslan skills) felt that comments about the staff members' inability to sign dismissed the value of those who had already developed Auslan skills. She also worried that her peers might be content to allow the program to hinge on whether a Deaf person would seek employment at the school: "I'm worried that it is just going to fall in a heap, and nothing is going to be done, or we are going to lose interest after a while because people keep knocking it down, saying we haven't got resources. I think [we should] start with the resources we have got" (12).

The next stage in the school's consideration of a bilingual program was to plan a visit to a site that resembled their own. Of those they could visit, they opted for an interstate program based in a school most similar to their own: a deaf facility within a regular school, in which teachers had transitioned from Total Communication to a bilingual policy several years earlier. However, even though the school community had agreed to make the visit, progress again stalled. Several of the teachers felt there was little they could do until the visit took place, whereas others were impatient to begin learning Auslan and saw no reason to delay. The facility coordinator was conscious that some members of the school community were more ready than others to go ahead with the transition: "I think we're still grappling with an understanding, you know. Even though the signs I'm getting from the staff are 'Yes, it's all go,' I still think we're all at different levels of understanding, and therefore if you don't fully understand what you're looking at, it's difficult to plan. . . . I think we've come a long way, but at the same time I think we've also got an awful long way to go" (9).

By the third and final interviews, there was widespread support for Auslan among the teachers and general agreement that the traditional way of educating deaf children had failed. Teachers who had at first had little or no knowledge of Auslan now believed it was more effective than Signed English. Although some were unclear about *how* a bilingual program would be introduced in their setting, there were calls for the systematic adoption of Auslan throughout the facility: "I think we would all agree that our communication skills are probably not adequate to the job that we're expected to do. . . . We should all be using the same system, and that should be using Auslan" (11).

When the time came for the two-day visit to the interstate bilingual program, thirteen teachers and parents made the trip. They observed and interacted with both deaf and hearing students and discussed their concerns with like-minded people in a similar school environment. On their return, they prepared a strategy for establishing a bilingual program and decided to begin with the primary school and extend the program into the secondary and senior-secondary schools as the children progressed.

Apple Hills worked quickly to establish bilingual education. After only eight months the teachers and parents had endorsed a bilingual education policy and secured funding to employ Deaf staff members. The following year the school hired two Deaf native Auslan users on a full-time basis, and a group of parents and teachers made a return visit to the interstate bilingual program.

Implications of the Study

Several factors facilitated the changes that occurred. First and foremost was the coordinator's strong leadership, which had the effect of legitimizing and endorsing the proposal. The study participants described him as a "solution-orientated" person who was open to the views of others. After many years' experience in deaf education, he recognized the need for improvement and set about investigating the options. His confidence in the direction he was taking the school was buoyed by the national and international movement toward bilingual deaf education and the growing number of Victorian schools that were including Auslan in their curricula. Throughout the study he remained optimistic that—with the backing of most of the parents—the school would be able to introduce a bilingual program. He stressed the importance of respecting the rights of other members of the school community and allowed teachers and parents to make up their own minds without feeling pressured. He also understood that some of the parents would oppose a change but did not fall back on this as a reason for *not* taking action. His decision to support this study was viewed as an indication of the undeniable *need* for change.

The second significant factor is that this study coincided with the teachers' readiness for change. Their dissatisfaction with the students' progress and their disappointment with established practices prompted them to question the efficacy of their methods and consider new ones. They responded openly to discussions about language policy, did not defend old practices, and did not blame deafness for their students' educational underachievement. Instead, they questioned *their own* practices without locating the deficit or disability in the children, unlike most other teachers from oral or TC settings (see Komesaroff 1998). Several Apple Hills teachers pointed to their involvement in this study as having influenced their own beliefs and thus the changes that occurred in their school. The study provided them with a rationale for modifying existing practices and a model for new ones. A teacher who already had established views

about the inadequacy of instructing deaf students through spoken and/
or Signed English felt that I was in a better position—as an outsider—to
effect change. Indeed, he commented that "you can't achieve enormous
change by yourself. . . . You need other people working with you—
people who are like-minded and people who are all heading in the same
direction" (11).

Garnering the parents' support was essential. They were given time
and opportunity to learn about Auslan and bilingual education, to observe
Auslan being used in the classroom, and to witness their children's responses. Without Auslan skills, teachers are not in a position to provide
this modeling, and they themselves need to see bilingual pedagogy in action. Working alongside teachers in their classrooms was a powerful influence on their acceptance of new language practices. Several teachers
and parents had assumed Auslan would be inaccessible to their children,
given their lack of prior contact with native or fluent signers. The children's positive response to Auslan and Deaf adults forced them to reas-
sess their beliefs and dispelled the misconception that deaf children raised
without exposure to native sign language cannot learn Auslan. It was important for the teachers and parents to observe deaf children with age-
appropriate linguistic skills, such as those raised with Auslan in bilingual
settings or Deaf families. Employing Deaf staff members who were native
or fluent Auslan users provided the school community with linguistic
role models and a positive view of deafness.

Expecting teachers to acquire Auslan while on the job, however, is
problematic. Without Auslan, teachers have little option other than
using English (spoken and/or signed). The difficulty they will face in
acquiring a new language is an understandable disincentive to changing
language policy and practice. The teachers in this study identified their
need for regular classes, Auslan immersion, and regular contact with native signers. Teachers who are in the midst of bringing about significant
changes in both their school's language policy and their personal language skills clearly need support. It may be too late to expect schools to
provide the professional development necessary to ensure that teachers
become fluent in Auslan. In addition, this level of training may well go
beyond the resources of many schools. The changes must begin in
teacher education and professional development programs to ensure that

Australian teachers of deaf children are proficient in Auslan and competent in bilingual pedagogy. Failure to do so perpetuates the use of English, without providing any real choice in the language to be used to instruct deaf children.

The federal government of Australia contributes substantially to education in the states, but it is the managers of the state departments of education and the ministers of education who manage the system (see http://www.icponline.org/feature_articles/f19_02.htm [accessed August 11, 2003]). When Apple Hills and other bilingual programs for deaf students were being established in the late 1990s, the senior managers in the Victorian Department of Education whom I interviewed showed no evidence of having considered bilingual education. Four of them stated that the need for bilingual programs had not been mentioned to them, and three of these four reported that they had not heard of Auslan and were unfamiliar with the term *bilingual* in conjunction with deaf education. The one senior manager who was aware of the debate called it "peripheral" (Komesaroff 1998, 149) and an "internal school issue" (ibid., 150). These managers regarded senior TODs as leaders in the field who should be informing them of any critical issues in deaf education.

With the increased autonomy of Victorian schools in the past decade and the lack of leadership from Department of Education managers, the coordinators or principals of programs for deaf students have been in a strong position to either initiate or resist change. The result has been that most Australian bilingual programs for deaf students, such as the one at Apple Hills, have been created by a policy change at the school level.

CHAPTER 5

———

Parents Take Their Fight to the Courts

The road to infraction of discrimination law, as to other places to be avoided, may be paved with good intentions.

—*The Honorable Justice Madgwick in Clarke v. CEO*

SINCE THE 1990s a small but growing number of deaf children have had access to bilingual programs in most states of Australia. These programs have continued to exist within a system that predominantly integrates deaf children into regular schools and instructs them by means of the oral or Total Communication approaches. A central platform of the Australian education policy for students with special needs is the parents' right to choose the educational setting for their child. However, the *language* of instruction to which a deaf child has access may be less a matter of parental choice, particularly if that language is Auslan.

Antidiscrimination Legislation

Australia's human rights policy is based on the principle that human rights are "inherent, inalienable, indivisible and universal" (Commonwealth of

Australia [CoA], 2005a, 5). Moreover, "they are the birthright of all human beings, cannot be lost or taken away, are all of equal importance and apply to all persons irrespective of race, sex, disability, language, religion, political or other opinion, national or social origin, age, property or other status" (ibid.). In addition, "in those states in which ethnic, religious or linguistic minorities exist, persons belonging to such minorities shall not be denied the right, in community with the other members of their group, to enjoy their own culture, to profess and practice their own religion, or to use their own language" (Ruddock 2004, 81).

Although the right of linguistic minorities in Australia to use their language "in community with others" is protected, the right to access that language in education has not been made explicit. Antidiscrimination law in Australia is based on four federal acts:

- Human Rights and Equal Opportunity Commission Act of 1986
- Racial Discrimination Act of 1975
- Sex Discrimination Act of 1984
- Disability Discrimination Act of 1992

The Australian Disability Discrimination Act (DDA) (Cth) 1992 (CoA 1992) makes it unlawful to discriminate, directly or indirectly, against a person on the grounds of a disability, as well as against an associate of a person with a disability.[1] The act covers many areas of public life including "employment, education, provision of goods, services, and facilities, access to premises, accommodation, clubs and incorporated associations, dealing with land, sport, and in the administration of Commonwealth laws and programs" (Human Rights and Equal Opportunity Commission 2003). Under Section 22 of the act, it is unlawful for an educational authority to discriminate against a student on the grounds of disability by (1) refusing or failing to accept an application for admission or in the terms or conditions on which admission is made; (2) denying or limiting access to

---

1. "Disability" is defined as a physical, intellectual, psychiatric, sensory, neurological, or learning impairment; physical disfigurement; or the presence of disease-causing organisms in the body.

any benefit provided by the authority; or (3) expelling or subjecting the student to any other detriment.

In March 2005 Parliament passed the Disability Discrimination Amendment (Education Standards) Act. The purpose of formulating disability standards for education is to clarify and make more explicit both the rights of people with disabilities and the obligations of education service providers and to avoid unlawful discrimination. The amendment extends the defense of "unjustifiable hardship" to aspects of education beyond the point of enrollment, clarifies the position of education providers with respect to "reasonable adjustments," and provides guidance to education providers on how to meet their obligations to students with disabilities. For example, students should be provided with access to services on the same basis as students without a disability. The education standards also make explicit the need for education providers to ensure students' access through measures that include "appropriately trained support staff, such as specialist teachers, interpreters, note-takers and teachers' aides" (CoA 2005b, 21). The development of the education standards took seven and a half years and was finally completed after a 2002 committee of inquiry highlighted the urgent need for nationally consistent disability standards for education (Regulation Impact Statement, 27, at www.ag.gov/DSFE; accessed March 30, 2005). It remains to be seen whether the introduction of these standards will reduce the incidence of discrimination and avoid future legal action by parents of deaf children.

Under the DDA a complaint may be filed with the Australian Human Rights and Equal Opportunity Commission (HREOC), after which the parties go through a process of conciliation. The president of HREOC can terminate a complaint of alleged unlawful discrimination in a number of situations, including those that present no reasonable prospect of settlement during intervention (Ruddock 2004). Settlement is reached in 30–35 percent of all cases (based on statistics for the last three reported periods, 2000–2003; HREOC 2005b), although it may be reached without either admission of liability or a requirement of confidentiality (Komesaroff 2003). Doing so avoids setting legal precedent.

If conciliation fails or the complaint of unlawful discrimination is otherwise terminated, the complainant has the right to take action in the federal court. In these cases, the presiding judge has the power to (a) direct the respondent not to repeat or continue the discrimination,

(b) order the respondent to perform any reasonable act or course of conduct to redress any loss or damage, (c) require a respondent to employ or reemploy an applicant, and (d) order the respondent to pay damages by way of compensation (Ruddock 2004). If the discrimination is the result of a condition or requirement that is unreasonable, disproportionately affects people with a disability, or is impossible for a person with a disability to comply with, then it is deemed to be "indirect discrimination." The largest group of complaints received by the HREOC are related to the DDA. In 2002 and 2003, the commission received 493 complaints (40 percent of all complaints) related to disability.

The percentage of disability complaints in education is also growing—8 percent in 2000 and 2001, 9 percent in 2001 and 2002, and 11 percent in 2002 and 2003. The DDA is considered to have been more effective in the area of education than elsewhere (see the Disability Standards for Education 2004 Regulation Impact Statement at www.ag.gov.au). Since 2000, on average 2.8 percent of disability complaints in all areas (employment, goods and services, accommodation, education, sports, and so on) have been brought by deaf people. A further 3.8 percent of all disability complaints relate to the separate category of "hearing impaired":[2] Most of the education complaints involve universities and government primary schools (Toohey and Hurwitz 2002). About half of these cases are resolved through conciliation.

The Complaints

The HREOC does not release the number of complaints related to deafness and education. However, through searches of its complaints log and mediated outcomes, as well as my involvement as an expert witness, I found at least ten cases that have been filed, mediated, or continued to a hearing or court proceeding since the introduction of the DDA in 1992. A growing number of complaints have been made against education

---

2. HREOC annual reports, available at http://www.hreoc.gov.au/complaints_information/ statistics/index.html, accessed March 30, 2005. For related discussion of the law and special educational needs see Henshaw (2003), and for a discussion of disability discrimination in Australia and New Zealand see Varnham (2003).

authorities over the absence of Auslan in programs for deaf children. The authorities have defended their methods of instruction and support, which have included Signed English, Total Communication, and note taking. While some cases resulted in confidential settlements, others failed during intervention and were either withdrawn or heard by a higher legal jurisdiction. The complainants alleged discrimination on the basis of their child's lack of access to Auslan in the classroom due to an absence of qualified interpreters, qualified teachers proficient in Auslan, and/or support staff fluent in Auslan. Each of the education-related complaints is summarized here:

> Complaint 1: In 1995 deaf parents filed a complaint against a segregated school for deaf children in Victoria and the state department of education. The case was withdrawn in 1997.
>
> Complaint 2: In 1999 the mother of a deaf boy alleged that her son had been discriminated against in the facilities the State of New South Wales provided for her son. While the school acknowledged the child's use of Auslan signs "and natural gestures," the mother claimed that it had failed to provide him with accessible linguistic models, which resulted in a delay in the child's acquisition of language (witness statement, Komesaroff, December 9, 1999). The complaint was withdrawn as a result of the mother's death, despite the expediting of the hearing (see HREOC 2000).
>
> Complaint 3: In 1993 a statewide parent support group filed a complaint that claimed that the education department was deficient in providing services to deaf students. The group formally called for the provision of bilingual/bicultural education as an educational option. A mediated outcome was reached in 1997. When a working group of both parties was established to discuss issues of concern at biannual meetings, the participants decided that the parent support group would provide feedback and advice to the department on matters of individual concern to parents and that the support group would contact the Board of Studies with regard to introducing Auslan as a subject in the senior years of secondary school (which confers the School Certificate and the Higher School Certificate) (HREOC 2005b).
>
> Complaint 4: Before 2000, a deaf secondary school student filed a complaint that alleged that her school had discriminated against her

by refusing to provide a sign language interpreter for her final-year exams. The case was dismissed. The commissioner denied the complaint on the basis that the school's actions were not unlawful, given that the school provided an oral program in a segregated setting (HREOC, updated 2000).

Complaint 5: The parents of a deaf child who had been taught in Auslan in a preschool program filed a complaint sometime between 1999 and 2001. The child was ready to begin formal education in a small regional school, but none of the teachers there were certified in Auslan. The department had offered part-time assistance through an aide who understood Auslan, but the child's parents were concerned that part-time access would disadvantage their daughter. A mediated outcome was reached. The department reviewed its policies and offered an incentive to qualified Auslan-fluent teachers to move to regional and remote areas. One was appointed prior to the beginning of the child's first year of formal schooling (Toohey and Hurwitz 2002).

Complaint 6: In 2000 the parents of a profoundly deaf girl who attended a local primary school alleged that the education department had failed to provide reasonable accommodation for their daughter because it had not employed an Auslan interpreter. They claimed that their daughter's educational opportunities were being wasted as she could not participate in the curriculum without an interpreter. A mediated outcome was reached, whereby the department created a new position for a full-time Auslan interpreter (HREOC 2005b).

Complaint 7: In 2002 the mother of a seven-year-old profoundly deaf girl who communicates through Auslan maintained that her daughter could not access educational services on equal terms with other children because the state school at which she was enrolled had not provided an interpreter or a teacher with Auslan skills. A mediated outcome was reached. Reasonable adjustment was provided, and a change in policy and practice was instituted (HREOC 2002).

At least two other complaints were filed with the HREOC in which the parties reached a confidential settlement, but no details are available. The following section provides a fuller description of two of these complaints in order to provide insights into the process and broader context of each case.

Complaint 1: Withdrawn

In 1996 two Deaf and two hearing parents filed a complaint (on behalf of other parents at their children's school) against a school for deaf children and the Victorian Department of Education. The parents had been actively lobbying local and state education authorities for a bilingual program at their children's school. As members of the school council and its education subcommittee, they attempted to bring about change within the school; when this failed they addressed formal complaints to the school principal, school board, governing board, district liaison principal, minister of education, and state premier before seeking legal action.

The parents claimed indirect discrimination because of the school's unwillingness to establish a bilingual program in which Auslan would be utilized as their children's first language and as the language of instruction in the classroom. Without this program, they said, their children were being denied full access to education. Their decision to file the complaint followed years of dissatisfaction with and frustration over the absence of Auslan in the classroom and the continued use of Signed English despite the parents' wishes. They were highly critical of the lack of information given to the school community about the benefits of bilingual education, the lack of effort to introduce parents to Deaf adults, and the teachers' failure to recognize the advantage of educating deaf students in their native sign language. They also alleged that the school principal had actively ignored their requests for a bilingual program, encouraged parents to place their children in the school's oral program instead, and warned them against the use of Auslan (claiming it would not develop their child's literacy skills). When one of the parents (who was herself a qualified teacher) tabled a formal request for teachers to use Auslan at a meeting of the school board and governing board, she was told that she failed to realize the benefits of Signed English for her child. The complaint against the school included the following claims:

- The students had limited or no access to instruction through Auslan.
- Signed English was used *counter to* the parents' wishes.
- There was a lack of certified teachers who were proficient or accredited in the use of Auslan.

- The staff members who were proficient in Auslan were not certified teachers.
- The lack of Auslan interpreters limited the children's (and Deaf parents') access to the school's programs and community activities.
- The school employed integration aides who did not have Auslan skills.
- The school was continuing to recruit and employ staff members who had *no* Auslan skills.
- The school actively discouraged the use of Auslan and pressured the parents *not* to use it as well.
- Parents were advised to integrate their children into regular schools (rather than place them in an affiliated school for deaf children) after leaving the program.
- The program relied on charitable bequests and thus ran the risk of financial shortfalls each year.

To strengthen their complaint, the parents documented the inadequate access their children had to Auslan in the classroom. Despite their requests, the Auslan-qualified teacher instructed in Signed English. Beginning in 1992 a Deaf adult who was employed as an integration aide interacted with the children in Auslan for as little as half a day every week. In 1993 the position increased to three days a week and in 1995 became a full-time position. During the first three years of the program, the children had no access to Auslan whatsoever on the days the integration aide was not scheduled to work. They also cited examples of the inaccessibility of school events, at which no Auslan interpreters were available, such as sports days and concerts. They requested greater recognition of Auslan and its introduction as a language of instruction in the "bilingual" class, the appointment of qualified teachers accredited in Auslan, preservice and in-service training in Auslan for TODs. They also called for all TODs in the state to be proficient in Auslan.

The case lasted an extremely long time due to administrative errors in processing the complaint and ongoing problems maintaining legal representation. Formal attempts to reach agreement through mediation did not begin until almost two years after the complaint was filed. When intervention meetings were finally scheduled, the principal and the

department representatives denied all aspects of the complaint and refused all of the parents' requests. The complaint was therefore slated for
a hearing at the HREOC.

After several months, the legal firm that had taken on the case pro
bono claimed a "conflict of interest" and referred the parents to the
Public Interest Law Clearing House (PILCH), an independent, not-for-
profit, legal referral service.[3] Again the same thing happened, and after
months of preparation the parents were again referred to PILCH to meet
with their third group of legal representatives. Their meeting with the
barrister who had agreed to represent them did not go well. The parents
sensed little support for or understanding of their case and were advised
to think seriously about whether to proceed with the complaint. After
more than four years of legal wrangling and realizing that the judgment
might go against them, they reluctantly withdrew the complaint. Having
completed the junior grades, their children were no longer at the school
in question, and the state department had unexpectedly contributed funds
to improve students' access to Auslan at the school. Thus the parents may
have been viewed as pursuing an egregious complaint. Furthermore, in
the four years it had taken for their complaint to be processed, legislative
changes had been made that meant that the HREOC (a state agency)
could no longer hear such cases. Complaints filed under federal law,
such as the DDA, had to be heard by the Federal Court of Australia,
where costs could be awarded against the unsuccessful party.

Although this case did not go to hearing, it appeared to have some positive effects on the school's access to state resources. The state department
contributed funds to secure students' access to Auslan in the bilingual program and commissioned a research study to evaluate the school's program.
Unfortunately, the broader structural changes the parents sought to ensure
that deaf children in Victoria had access to Auslan were not made, and
further complaints were brought against the state education department.
One resulted in a confidential settlement just prior to the court hearing.

---

3. The Public Interest Law Clearing House "seeks to meet the legal needs of community
groups, not for profit organisations and individuals from disadvantaged or marginalised
backgrounds. PILCH acts as a facilitator for the community to access pro bono legal
assistance from the private legal profession" (http://www.pilch.org.au/html/default.asp;
accessed June 6, 2007).

Complaint 3: Mediated Outcome

In 1993 a statewide parent support group—the Parent Council for Deaf Education (PCDE)—filed a complaint under the DDA against the New South Wales Department of School Education (DSE), now known as the Department of Education and Training. The complaint followed unsuccessful attempts in New South Wales (NSW) in the early 1990s to establish a bilingual program for deaf students in government schools (Graham 1994).[4] The parent council claimed the department had failed to provide equal access to education for deaf students because most of the teachers and students in regular schools could not communicate with deaf students, many of the teachers who had signing students in their classes did not have adequate communication skills, there was an inadequate number of suitably qualified interpreters, and students who were graduating from government schools were essentially illiterate (Friedlander 1993).

The PCDE (1996, 31) claimed that "the Department is routinely forcing hearing disabled students into situations where they are taught by people they cannot understand." It reported a general lack of access to Auslan in deaf education in NSW government schools and asserted that the state education authority had ignored longitudinal studies from bilingual programs in other countries. The PCDE formally called for the provision of bilingual/bicultural education as an educational option in NSW (ibid.) and identified six deficiencies in the services the DSE was providing to deaf students:

1. an insufficient number of qualified interpreters
2. an inadequate number of qualified teachers of deaf children
3. ad hoc provision of resources and personnel funding for deaf students integrated into regular schools
4. absence of a segregated secondary school for deaf students using sign language
5. lack of support for the promotion and understanding of deaf students by their hearing peers

---

4. The first bilingual programs in New South Wales were established in private institutions.

6. absence of bilingual/bicultural programs for deaf students in the government sector

Four years after the complaint was filed, the parties reached a mediated solution. They agreed to the establishment of a working group that would convene biannual meetings, in which both parties would discuss issues of concern and the PCDE representatives could provide feedback and advice to the department on matters of concern. The PCDE could also contact the Board of Studies with regard to introducing Auslan as a final-year subject in NSW schools (HREOC 2005b).

However, the agreement did little to resolve the parents' concerns or provide a solution to deaf children's lack of access to Auslan in NSW government schools. One year after the agreement was signed, the PCDE newsletter commented, "We are a long way from achieving a workable outcome given the policies and bureaucracy that is [*sic*] found in a large Government Department such as the DSE" (PCDE 1998, 5).

Complaints That Went before a Court

In my experience, the decision to file a formal complaint of discrimination against education authorities is not taken lightly. Significant costs, both human and monetary, are involved, and a long period of uncertainty ensues until a judgment is rendered. The decision to file usually follows repeated, unsuccessful requests to teachers, administrators, and state education authorities to institute changes. In some cases, the mere threat of legal action has been sufficient to prompt education authorities to respond to parents' requests (witness cited in Case 2, 2004, para. 596); in others, even a ruling made in the federal court against the education authorities is not sufficient to convince them of the need to change. Such was the situation in three cases, two of which were heard by the Federal Court of Australia (the complaints having been filed under the DDA); the third was heard by the Victorian Civil and Administrative Tribunal (VCAT) (the complaint having been filed under the Equal Opportunity Act of 1995):

1. *Clarke v. Catholic Education Office and Another*

2. *Hurst and Devlin v. Education Queensland*
3. *Beasley v. Victorian Department of Education, Employment, and Training*

The way in which the respondents argued *against* the use of Auslan in these cases is of particular interest. I analyzed the proceedings and the decisions, as all were published on government websites or were available in electronic databases. My focus was the views of Auslan presented to the court by the defense lawyers and expert witnesses on cross-examination. Given the obligation for legal counsel to act within the broad parameters of the client's instructions, this analysis provides valuable insight into how Auslan is understood by education authorities and/ or represented to the courts.

Case 1. *Clarke v. Catholic Education Office and Another*

In *Clarke v. Catholic Education Office and Another* the parents of eleven-year-old Jacob Clarke filed a complaint against the Australian Capital Territory Catholic Education Office (an independent education authority) and McKillop Secondary College. Jacob's parents claimed discrimination with regard to the terms and conditions on which the school was prepared to enroll their son and the requirement or condition of enrollment that he participate in and receive instruction *without* the use of an Auslan interpreter. The basis of the charge was the allegedly unreasonable inadequacy of the model of support the respondents offered (*Catholic Education Office v. Clarke* [2004] FCAFC 197, para. 8).[5]

The secondary college had made an offer of enrollment on the basis that Jacob receive note-taking support with the *possibility* of some access to signing. Jacob's parents offered the school a grant of $15,000 as contingency funds for an interpreter if government funds were not made available. However, the model of support offered to Jacob provided only conditional use of Auslan "*if* a staff member . . . were to have these skills and be in a position to input into the learning support program . . . *if possible*, [to] have . . . *peers* from . . . his year 7 classes to support him

---

5. Hereafter referred to as Case 1 (2004).

with interpreting and relaying verbal messages (Case 1, 2003, para. 15; emphasis added).

Jacob's parents submitted to the court that the primary support offered by the school was note-taking and that access to Auslan was no more than a possibility. Nothing suggested that the college accepted Jacob's need for signing support or that the respondents would actively seek such assistance. The parents claimed that the evidence indicated an absence of an intention to provide the necessary aid (Case 1, 2003, para. 64).

Despite the unanimous agreement that Jacob needed an interpreter while in court, the defense and its key expert witness nevertheless argued that Jacob would be able to participate in school without a sign language interpreter. The witness (W), a qualified teacher of deaf students and the special needs consultant for the Catholic Education Office (CEO), stated that "Jacob is a bright boy who has very good strategies for getting information. If he gets it through signing, as well as signing support, then it is easier for him, but he can get information by other means as well" (Case 1, 2002, Day 2, 52).

The respondents, represented by defense counsel Bain, Queen's Counsel (QC),[6] denied the allegation of unlawful discrimination by asserting the following:

1. [Jacob was] a total communicator and not Auslan dependent and whilst it may have been easier for him to have Auslan, the other non-Auslan strategies would nevertheless have enabled him to participate in classroom instruction;
2. The long-term goal, agreed on all hands, was for Jacob to be an independent learner and to live as fully as possible in a hearing, that is, non-Auslan world;
3. The model of support was based on expert advice and consideration of both professional and personal opinions, including those of the Clarkes, and was either suitable for Jacob or reasonably thought to be so;

----

6. Queens Counsel (QC) are barristers who are designated "one of Her Majesty's counsel learned in the law," an appointment that the Crown confers and the courts recognize.

4. It was understood that . . . [no] staff with signing/Auslan skills would be available at the College;

5. The availability of resources to assist Jacob and the shortage of Auslan-trained assistants for teachers was not unlimited;

6. The Clarkes' offer of a grant could not be accepted because of potential inequity issues concerning families other than the Clarkes and possible future funding consequences (government might consider that the CEO was able to raise its own funds and did not require as much financial assistance as might be presently available); and

7. The agreed model of support at no stage ruled out the possibility of signing support, including Auslan support, and the respondents intended to pursue (as their actions, in actively pursuing, showed) throughout 1999, a range of options, including signing, as part of an overall and evolving model of support. (Case 1, 2003, para. 55)

In what I have elsewhere called "fuzzy logic" (Komesaroff 2005), Witness W claimed that the *absence* of an interpreter in the classroom would provide Jacob with an opportunity to "learn the strategies for coping in the wider community, which is a hearing community, and go on to university, to tertiary [education], where it's not a closed deaf community" (Witness W in Case 1, 2002, Day 2, 53). Under cross-examination by legal counsel (LC) for the applicants, Witness W then claimed that Jacob spoke English, despite the unintelligibility of his speech heard the previous day in court (ibid., 55; emphasis added):[7]

LC: One of the aspects of total communication, which you refer to in your evidence . . . is that Jacob can speak English?

W: Yes.

---

7. At one point Jacob uttered the word "yes," without the use of sign language. The judge asked what he had said and requested that Jacob sign his testimony so that it could be interpreted for the court. It was clear that even the use of a simple one-word spoken response in context was unintelligible to the judge.

LC: Yes, now did you see him attempting to speak English yesterday here?

W: Yes.

LC: And did you consider that was understandable?

W: I've got a very well tuned ear for deaf children's speech, and, yes, I could understand him.

LC: Yes. For people who don't have well tuned ears to deaf speech, it wasn't understandable, was it?

W: But *he's still speaking English whether you can understand it or not.*

LC: Well, if he's attempting to communicate with a person who doesn't understand it, then he's not communicating, is he? Would you agree with that?

W: *He is communicating. . . . The other person may not be able to receive that communication, but he is attempting to communicate* in English.

Jacob's parents alleged that this witness had advised Jacob's grade 6 teacher against learning Auslan so that Jacob would have the opportunity of being with someone who *could not* communicate through sign language. As members of a linguistic minority, deaf children are surrounded by hearing people who cannot communicate through sign language; hence, the lack of logic of this witness's recommendation.

The Honorable Justice Madgwick ruled in favor of Jacob's parents. The CEO appealed Justice Madgwick's ruling in federal court, where a three-judge panel affirmed that the Catholic Education Office and MacKillop Catholic College had unlawfully discriminated against Jacob Clarke by failing to offer Auslan support. Damages of $26,000 were awarded to Jacob as compensation (Case 1, 2004).

Justice Madgwick's comments on this case are particularly instructive. Despite the defense counsel's best efforts to discount Jacob's need for Auslan and to blur the distinction between native sign language and Total Communication, the justice saw clearly that "whatever the hopes may have been, having seen Jacob at 14, it must have been pretty clear to skilled people when he was 11 that he was not going to go far without Auslan" (Case 1, 2002, 38–39). In deciding the case he added, "Jacob's parents were clearly right in their assessment of Jacob's short term needs. . . . Jacob's need at the time was for Auslan support" (Case 1, 2003, para. 63).

Justice Madgwick determined that the main issue of contention in this case, from a legal point of view, was what could be considered *reasonable* for a child assessed as profoundly deaf. "It is not in dispute between the parties that Jacob required assistance and that the respondents should have provided it," he noted. "In the end, the question comes down to whether, in all the circumstances, the type of assistance the respondents offered was reasonable (ibid., para. 4).

Justice Madgwick dismissed the argument made by the defense that Jacob could successfully communicate *without* Auslan, that he should no longer depend on an Auslan interpreter, and that it was unreasonable to provide him with Auslan support:

> It is not the case . . . that, by using the totality of available means of attempted communication, Jacob successfully communicates without engaging in Auslan. Nor, in my judgment, is or was there any prospect of his being able to do so either quickly or without difficulty. The position would, at relevant times for judgment in this case, at least have been no better than that. Unless that is understood, the term "total communicator" is apt to be misleading. Jacob did not, in any adequate sense for most educational purposes, communicate without Auslan (ibid., para. 61).

> The view that Jacob should no longer depend on an interpreter was, on all the evidence before me, a wrong one. He could not simply forthwith cease such dependency. As indicated above, it is not enough that that view was wrong. The view was also, in my opinion, not a reasonable one. Jacob was quite dependent on Auslan. It should have been obvious to any adult that suddenly to separate him from that language in the classroom context would cause him distress, confusion and frustration: that is such separation would cause him harm. The situation was, as the respondents' agents should have known, not at all analogous to the immersion of a hearing speaker of a language into the milieu of another language with a view to learning the latter: Jacob cannot hear, his lip reading skills were limited, and his ability to draw inferences from the visual context was not well developed (ibid., para. 73).

> Auslan was not merely used in rare instances by deaf people. Nor was it, to say the least of it, an unreasonable aid for a deaf pupil, nor was

it in any way so special that it was incapable of being, at least partially, provided as a class room support for Jacob (ibid., para. 78).

Justice Madgwick also questioned the defense counsel's assertion that note-taking was an appropriate method of support for Jacob. "But that cannot be right," he said. "What is the child to do? Sit in the class watching the note taker? . . . I mean, a profoundly deaf—a profoundly deaf person?" (Case 1, 2002, 73). When the defense counsel (DC) suggested that it was appropriate to adopt this approach if a child communicates through speech and lipreading, Justice Madgwick questioned their logic (ibid., 76):

> JM: Yes, but does Jacob communicate through speech and lipreading?
> DC: Not as his—not as an adequate form of communication, no.
> JM: You see, that is the problem with the question.

Furthermore, he rejected the defense's argument that the school had merely been unable to promise Auslan support, given the uncertainty of government funding and the difficulty in locating suitably skilled staff (Case 1, 2002, Day 2). Rather, he observed that this did "not really sound like, 'We will be very happy to have signing if only we can get the money for it, but we cannot guarantee it.' . . . I get the impression clearly from this, there is a certain lack of enthusiasm for Auslan and signing" (ibid., 32–33).

In an exchange with the defense counsel, Justice Madgwick questioned the willingness of the school to respond to the parents' requests for Auslan (ibid., 35–36):

> JM: But it is not that there was a simple lack of meeting of minds; I do not think that for a second.
> DC: There was no philosophical objection to Auslan; there were impediments.
> JM: No, and no actual willingness to go out of their way to see it happen, which is what the case is about.
> DC: No, well . . .

JM: If Auslan fell in their lap, the Catholic system would be happy to
accept it. . . . There is all the difference in the world between saying, 'Look, great idea, terrific, all right, you find the people and
subject to money, we'll hire them.' That simple. Now that was
not being said.

In explaining his decision, Justice Madgwick acknowledged the dissen-
tion among educators in this field: "I approach this matter with some
caution, since it involves intrusion into a field where, on matters of principle, there is some division of views among experts" (Case 1, 2003,
para. 54). However, he also recognized the linguistic legitimacy of Auslan and its integrity as a language other than English (ibid., para. 5): "A
characteristic of Auslan is that it is not in any sense the translation of
English by manual signals into hand and finger movements, but is a
means of directly expressing perceptions, facts and ideas through the use
of hands and body gestures. It is a language in its own right albeit not a
spoken one: it has its own syntax, grammar, lexicon and devices to represent words."

Case 2. *Hurst and Devlin v. Education Queensland*

In *Hurst and Devlin v. Education Queensland* the parents of eleven-year-
old Ben Devlin and Tiahna Hurst filed a complaint against the state education authority, Education Queensland, that alleged indirect discrimination by the state because it had failed to provide their children with an
adequate education (Case 2, 2004).[8] The claim of discrimination was
made under sections 22a and 22c of the DDA, which makes it unlawful
to discriminate by limiting students' access to any benefit provided by

---

8. A joint complaint by two families, Hurst and Devlin, against Education Queensland
was filed and heard by the federal court, which ruled in favor of Devlin and against
Hurst, whose application was dismissed. The Hursts have filed an appeal, which the
federal court is likely to hear early in 2006. Data that relate only to Hurst have not been
cited in this book.

an educational authority or subjecting them to any other detriment. Ben, who was born profoundly deaf, was assessed as being severely language delayed. He had attended a local school, where he spent most mornings in a special education class, and worked in a modified education program in the afternoon, where he was mainstreamed into a regular class. Ben's parents pointed to the general lack of access to full-time Auslan interpreters in Queensland schools and the absence (at the time) of bilingual education programs for deaf children in the state government sector (http://www.auslancase.kpslawyers.com; accessed October 9, 2003).

The case was initially heard by the Honorable Justice Spender in March 2004. However, after several days' proceedings, during which several witnesses for the applicants gave evidence, Justice Spender recused himself "on the ground of a reasonable apprehension of bias" (Case 2, 2004, para. 1). Three months later the case returned to the federal court and was reheard by the Honorable Justice Lander.

The parents claimed that Ben had been taught by spoken and Signed English that was poor in quality and fluency and was an "inferior method of communication" (ibid., para. 112) in comparison with Auslan. The result, they claimed, was that Ben's education had been impeded because of the school's failure to provide him with teachers who were fluent in Auslan. The parents submitted to the court that Ben would have received a better education if his teachers had used Auslan and that Auslan was the only method of communication that should have been used with him.

In her opening remarks while representing Education Queensland, Felicity Hampel (QC) denied the allegation of unlawful discrimination and claimed that the state education policy recognized a variety of methods of communicating with deaf students: "Auslan is but one of the methods of communication recognized under the total communication [policy]" (*Hurst and Devlin v. Education Queensland* [2005] FAC 405, para. 115).[9] She pointed to a "divergence in relevant opinion" (para. 114) about the best method of communication when teaching deaf students and asserted that the education offered to Ben was in no way inferior to

---

9. Hereafter referred to as Case 2 (2005).

that offered to his hearing peers. Education Queensland considered any lack of educational progress made by a student to be unrelated to the teaching program. Instead, the reasons for any educational delay were attributable solely to the child or the child's parents, in particular with regard to the following issues:

- [the] delay in Ben's diagnosis
- [the] delay in introducing Ben to signing, at his parents' request
- Ben's poor behavior at times in class
- Ben's regular failure to perform homework tasks
- Ben's irregular school attendance
- Ben's regular failure to wear FM amplification at school
- the nonexistent signing skills (in either Auslan or Signed English) of Ben's parents and siblings (Case 2, 2005, para. 118 and para. 120)

Justice Lander determined that Education Queensland had discriminated against Ben Devlin by failing to instruct him through Auslan. Part of the damages included $40,000 in compensation for future loss of earning capacity equivalent to two years' of lost schooling "because of the failure of the Education Queensland to provide him with an Auslan teacher or interpreter" (ibid., para. 859).

In contrast to *Clarke v. Catholic Education Office and Another*, Justice Lander's ruling in this case is more difficult to analyze. First, part of his decision refers to the applicant Tiahna Hurst, whose case is being appealed, and therefore has been omitted from analysis. Second, Justice Lander included large portions of testimony from opposing sides of the case and made statements that appear to contradict his ruling. Third, he issued no order in relation to the state's future provision of educational support for Ben and instead expressed his view that educators should select the most appropriate method of instruction for profoundly deaf children.

Case 3. *Beasley v. Victorian Department of Education, Employment, and Training*

In *Beasley v. Victorian Department of Education, Employment, and Training*, a Deaf mother, on behalf of her son Dylan, filed a complaint with the

Equal Opportunity Commission, in which she claimed discrimination by the Department of Education and Training (DOE). This mother asserted that Dylan's communication needs were not adequately being met because he received only sporadic access to instruction through Auslan. She also stated that the method of communication generally used was not the optimal method for educating Dylan. It had not enabled him to reach his academic potential, had not made it possible for him to achieve scholastic success comparable to that of his hearing peers, and was not a recognized language.

Since negotiation had failed, the commission referred the complaint to the Victorian Civil and Administrative Tribunal in June 2004. In August 2004 the respondents requested that the VCAT dismiss the complaint (or parts of it) on the grounds that it was misconceived and vexatious and/ or an abuse of process. However, the complaint proceeded to hearing, although without five paragraphs of the Particular of Complaint.

Consistent with the view of the school as autonomous, all of the managers made it clear that the DOE would not instigate changes to language practices in schools for deaf students. They viewed the debate as a methodological argument over *communication* rather than a broader issue of *language* policy. Schools are expected to take responsibility for resolving what managers in the Department of Education see as a professional debate: "The Department's view is quite clear. We do not discriminate between one language modality to another. We basically believe that if it can be organized at the local level to provide choice, then it should be. . . . We can't and don't dictate one [method] over the other and the Department is very clear about that, will not make a stand on that" (Komesaroff 1998, 148).

The department's policy of providing choice in deaf education must be questioned, given the lack of Auslan training available for teachers of deaf students. The first Victorian program, which was established in 1993, employed a Deaf teacher who used Auslan to work alongside a hearing teacher of deaf children who instructed through Signed English (Victorian School for Deaf Children 1993). In other Victorian programs, hearing teachers have continued to instruct through Signed English, while deaf adults, usually on a part-time basis, have served as Auslan models. Auslan signs have been used either in English word order in an approach called "Auslan-based signing" (see Moore 1997) or simultaneously with spoken English (see Coleman, Walsh, Pavia, Leane, and Bartlett 2000).

Defending Traditional Practices

In responding to these complaints, the education authorities have vigorously defended the efficacy of traditional practices and disagreed with the claims that these children have a right to access education through native sign language in their schools. The added qualification ("these" and "in their schools") smacks of a "NIMBY" (Not in My Back Yard) attitude, as Auslan is acknowledged as a community language but not accepted for use in their schools—or at least not to the extent that the power structures could be disrupted. It is instructive to analyze the way in which Auslan was represented to the courts in these cases and the arguments the respondents employed to defend the continuing use of English or English-based sign systems in their schools.

In the first two cases, the school systems (mis)represented the Total Communication (TC) approach by stating that it naturally included the use of Auslan. In the first case, the respondents to the complaint claimed that Jacob was a "Total Communicator"—someone, they said, who was capable of communicating independently through a variety of communication methods.

Similarly, in the second case, Education Queensland reported to the court that its TC policy *recognized a variety of methods of communication.* A witness for the defense, a senior manager in the state education department, testified that "Auslan is but one of the methods of communication recognized under the total communication [policy]" (Case 2, 2005, para. 115). However, this was not (nor has it since become) the department's policy. The Education Manual posted on the department's website clearly communicates the state policy that instruction for *all* students be provided in English: "English is the language of instruction for all students in Queensland schools. For those deaf/hearing impaired students requiring a signed component, Signed English is used as the method of instruction to develop communication and literacy skills" (Department of Education and the Arts [formerly Education Queensland] 2002, para. 2.13).

The defense counsel dismissed the international literature cited to support the applicants' case because of what he called Europe's "diet of bilinguality or multilinguality" (Case 2, 2004, Day 1, 114). He stated that in Sweden, for example, it was the "mainstream" policy for students to be taught in Swedish and English and, therefore, "in that sense, they have a multilinguality that is already in place, not to do with the efficiency or otherwise of signing in one way rather than signing in another way" (ibid.).

The respondents in the first case repeatedly devalued Auslan by referring to it in deficit terms and by establishing Auslan and English as binary opposites. The defense argued that Jacob Clarke was "Auslan dependent" (Case 1, 2002, Day 2, 66) and that reliance on sign language interpreters (if they were to be provided) would not be in his best interests.

In the second case, Auslan was primarily described by the features it *lacked* and its *deviance* from English. On Day 1 of the proceedings, the defense counsel referred to Auslan in the following ways:

- [It has] *no* aural [or oral] component . . . *no* written form . . . *doesn't have* things such as participial endings, plurals and other features of English morphology (Day 1, 74)
- [It makes] *heavy use of*—I won't say mannerisms but *gestures*, sometimes *gesticulation, facial expressions,* and other *unusual features* of ordinary spoken language to convey meaning and to convey expression
- [The] syntax *does not* follow English word order . . . [It is] *truly foreign* from English . . . [Its] difference [from English is] *extreme* . . . [It is] *not* the signs that are used for Signed English . . . [lacks] any common root stock [with English] (75)
- [It is] quite *confronting* . . . quite *foreign,* very *different* . . . lots of *exaggerated* facial expressions . . . *exaggerated* simply in a physical sense, and maybe for good purpose . . . gesture, even gesticulation, bodily movement . . . *no* sound, and an *unusual* . . . physical presentation (104)
- Parents, of course, aspire, as we've agreed, that [education has] got to be done in English, hasn't it? (108).

- If we have people who are being educated *as only* a deaf cohort . . .
  in Auslan, and those with whom they have to socialize or with
  whom they have to communicate not having Auslan, that is going
  to pose practical difficulties, isn't it? (109).

This negative view of Auslan was reiterated by expert witnesses for the
defense. Witness L, for instance, asserted the following:

- A child using Auslan *will not* automatically develop literacy in
  English, which is one of the major goals in schooling (Case 2,
  2005, para. 501)
- The use of Auslan itself does not guarantee acquisition of literacy
  skills (para. 507)
- Any student who uses Auslan, to the exclusion of all other methods of teaching, cannot acquire literacy in English (ibid., para.
  116)
- If a child is only educated in Auslan, then that child may not be able
  to communicate at all with that child's non-hearing impaired peers.
  That would retard the child's education insofar as it would affect
  the child's social interaction with other children (ibid., para. 555).

Witness P testified that it is "difficult to train an adult person who has
skills in Signed English in Auslan. Auslan is a separate language and, for
adults, it is like learning a *foreign* language. . . . It would be preferable to
train new teachers who were already fluent in Auslan. However, there
are very few candidates of that kind who could be trained as teachers"
(ibid., para. 497). He defended the state's delayed introduction of a bilingual (pilot) program, given the need to exercise caution. He considered it reasonable that Queensland lagged behind most other Australian
states in introducing a bilingual program because of the divergence of
opinion about method and the "absence of definitive research about the
success of the BLBC programs." He also suggested there were "difficulties associated with discontinuing a BLBC program after it had been
introduced . . . [and that] it could be quite detrimental to a child's education to have a BLBC program removed from a child once having been

introduced to it." Furthermore, there was a "relatively small number of students available to benefit from such a program" and "difficulty . . . finding a school willing to undertake the program" (ibid., para. 494).

Delays and Late Settlement

These cases exhibit a pattern of late settlement, in which *confidential* agreement is reached *immediately before* or during a hearing. Given the frequency with which departments of education make off-the-record arrangements, Elizabeth Hastings, a former state disability discrimination commissioner, questioned the motives of the education authorities:

> This pattern of late settlement is noteworthy and indicates that some education authorities are keen to avoid setting precedents in this area. In my opinion this ad hoc solution of individual cases is not the best way to make decisions: the important issues are not aired, discussed or determined, and our case law remains impoverished and unhelpful as to how to eliminate discrimination and thereby avoid complaints. (Hastings 1997)

My own view is similar to that of Hastings. I too question the intent of the education authorities, given the ongoing formal complaints about the absence of Auslan from the education of deaf children in Australia. Confidential conciliated settlements, made without an admission of liability, have avoided legal precedent and imposed a requirement of secrecy on some litigants. Beyond providing solutions to individual cases, they have done little to impose systematic change or alter the way in which future complaints are handled. Despite ongoing complaints, when Jacob Clarke's parents were seeking Auslan interpreters for their son, their attempts were "met with resistance": "We never really wanted to pursue this matter in the Courts. . . . We gave the CEO [Catholic Education Office] and MacKillop [school] ample opportunity to negotiate an outcome but all our attempts met with resistance. Jacob is profoundly deaf and uses AUSLAN as his first language. MacKillop was only prepared to offer a note-taker to support Jacob in the classroom. It should have been abundantly clear that Jacob would not have been able to cope in this circumstance" (press release, Nicholas Clarke, October 9, 2003).

Significance of the Complaints

True equality requires not identical treatment, but rather differential treatment in order to accommodate differential needs.
                                    —*De Groof and Lauwers 2002, 20*

The DDA provides the framework within which some parents of deaf children who have been denied instruction in Auslan have sought redress through the courts. The significance of these cases lies in the contribution they have made to Australian case law. Unlike with earlier complaints that were withdrawn or mediated or reached confidential settlement, decisions made by the federal court or other legal entities are accessible to the public and may be cited in future legal argument. However, the DDA operates within a system in which the development of case law is complaints driven: "The deficiency of a focus on individual complaints is the failure to address systemic discrimination. Further limitations of individual complaints are the delays, power imbalance between complainants and respondents, and 'burn out' of complainants" (Agostino 1999).

Justice Lander, who presided over the case *Devlin v. Education Queensland*, held the view that decisions about deaf education should be made by the educators because "the Court is not an expert on education and, more particularly, on the education of profoundly deaf children." However, Australian law generally acknowledges that the court is not an expert on any number of subjects, not only education; moreover, it is the role of expert witnesses to provide the court with this expertise. Furthermore, the DDA was intended to have an educative role and to promote social justice and attitudinal change:

I do not believe there is any better example of social justice than this legislation—legislation which provides the framework to eliminate the discrimination which prevents fair access for people with disabilities to jobs, education, sport and entertainment and which provides an effective means of overcoming perhaps the most significant barrier that people with disabilities face in this country—the attitudinal barrier. . . . The legislation would therefore perform an important educative role and would further social awareness and change. (Howe 1992)

The suggestion that decisions about language use in deaf education be left to teachers of deaf students fails to account for the situation in which the applicants found themselves: Their appeals for teachers to use Auslan were ignored or refused by those same teachers and/or school administrators. Without recourse to the courts, to whom do parents turn when their pleas for native sign language are ignored? On the basis of the evidence presented and the outcomes of the cases reported in this chapter, one cannot assume that TODs will necessarily make decisions in the best interests of those children.

Leaving decisions about Auslan use to teachers who lack knowledge or skills in that language is unlikely to protect the rights of deaf children for whom it is a first or preferred language. For evidence of teachers' resistance to change, we need look no further than a recent statement of competencies for TODs that was released by the Australian Association of Teachers of the Deaf (2005). The competency standards detail the skills and knowledge required of these teachers for qualification and certification. The standards state that teachers must "demonstrate an *understanding* of theories and communication approaches" (including Auslan and bilingual/bicultural approaches), but they do not require them to have any *demonstrated competence* in sign language (either native or contrived).

A second issue these cases raise is the unwillingness of some education providers to enable a child to access instruction through Auslan and their subsequent defense of this opposition in the name of educational efficacy. Faced with a child whose native or preferred language was Auslan, they failed to initiate the child's access to that language, refused to comply when asked by parents, were unable to negotiate an agreement when an official complaint was filed against them, defended their actions in court, and, in at least one case (*Clarke v. CEO*), unsuccessfully appealed the judge's ruling. Furthermore, even when five federal court judges (including three appeal judges) had ruled in favor of the applicants in two of these cases, future complaints were met with intransigence on the part of the education providers. This resistance to the use of native sign language in deaf education is in stark contrast to the official government recognition of Auslan as a community language and to the intentions of Australia's human rights policy (see DEET 1991; Ruddock 2004; CoA 2005a).

The final issue relates to the way in which the respondents, represented by legal counsel, argued against the use of Auslan in education. They defended their actions with profoundly deaf children from hearing families and brought in a witness who highlighted the importance of the parents' hearing status in decisions regarding the appropriate language for instruction: "Auslan is the natural language of Deaf children of Deaf parents who communicate using Auslan but cannot be considered the natural language of children born to hearing parents where it *is* not the language of the home (*Devlin v. Education Queensland* 2004, para. 501). . . . Children who best respond to such an approach [bilingual education] are deaf/hearing impaired children of deaf parents" (para. 506).

In both cases the children represented are from hearing families. It is perhaps unsurprising, however, that even when the child at the center of the complaint is from a Deaf family, the education providers still reject the use of Auslan as the language of instruction. Such was the case in a complaint that went before the Victorian Civil and Administrative Tribunal (Uebergang 2005).[10] The complainant, an eleven-year-old boy who attended a large deaf facility in a government primary school, claimed that none of his teachers or sign language interpreters could adequately communicate in Auslan. The boy was born profoundly deaf and has Deaf parents, an older deaf sibling, and an extended Deaf family. Auslan is his first language, yet the education providers rejected his claims that he would have been better taught in Auslan.

The cases described in this chapter are the first grievances related to the absence of Auslan in education to have gone before the federal court.

---

10. The hearing was scheduled to conclude in December 2005, after which time a decision would be made.

The rulings in favor of the applicants provide evidence of the rights of these children to access instruction through native sign language. These cases have also brought the issue of native sign language use in deaf education before the courts, thereby sending a strong message to education providers about the status of Auslan and the rights of deaf children and their families.

The continuing legal action taken by parents of deaf children since the introduction of the DDA suggests a failure of education authorities to adequately respond to the entreaties for bilingual programs in Australia. Since parents continue to face resistance to these requests, claims of "choice" in deaf education are merely rhetoric. Teachers and educational administrators need to be aware of the discriminatory practices that may exist within their own classrooms and schools. If litigation convinces them of this, then the legal fight is well worth their while. In the long run, however, legislation may be necessary to ensure that deaf children's linguistic rights are met.

A significant deficiency of complaints-based mechanisms, such as exist in Australian law, is the inadequacy of individual complaints to address systemic discrimination. Their limitations include delays, the power imbalance between complainants and respondents, "burn out" of complainants, and uncertainty because mediated settlements do not establish binding precedents (Agostino 1999).

CHAPTER 6

⁓

Linguistic Rights and Self-Determination

T HE CONVENTIONS OF THE United Nations provide guiding principles for the countries of the world. In 1924 the League of Nations adopted the first *Declaration of the Rights of the Child* (the Geneva Declaration), an international instrument that recognized the "vulnerable nature of childhood" (Mills 2007, 72). In 1959 the Geneva Assembly of the United Nations adopted the second *Declaration of the Rights of the Child*, thereby indicating "widespread acceptance of the idea that every individual, solely by virtue of being human, is entitled to enjoy human rights and freedoms" (ibid.).

The subsequent declaration, the *UN Convention on the Rights of the Child 1989,* set out the ways in which member states can protect and support children's rights by giving primary importance to the concept of "the best interests of the child" (ibid.). For example, children have the right to have their identity preserved "without unlawful interference" (Article 8), and children with disabilities, including deaf children, have the right to "enjoy a full and decent life, in conditions that ensure dignity, promote self-reliance and facilitate the child's active participation in the community" (Article 23). The declaration "recognizes them as participants in society in every aspect of their development and serves to protect their economic, social, cultural, civil, political and humanitarian rights by the process of codification. A feature of the Convention is its suite of 'guiding principles' which direct the way each right is to be fulfilled and respected. They serve as a constant reference for the implementation and monitoring of the rights of every child under the age of eighteen years set out in the 41 articles (paragraphs) of the Convention" (ibid.).

In addition to the convention, the United Nations passed a resolution that stated that "teachers and/or interpreters who are proficient in the indigenous sign language must be provided" in deaf education (United Nations 1989, 6). Several years later, during the United Nations Decade of Disabled Persons, UN Secretary General Boutros Boutros-Ghali (1995) supported the world Deaf community in its struggle for recognition of its linguistic rights by recognizing its right to sign language as its medium of communication.

The Standard Rules on the Equalization of Opportunities for Persons with Disabilities developed by the United Nations (hereafter referred to as the Standard Rules) promote equal opportunity and full participation in society for people with disabilities. Although the Standard Rules are only recommendations, they are intended to inform legislation and form the basis of plans of action for governments and organizations.

United Nations Commission on Human Rights Resolution 1998/31 strengthens the Standard Rules as an instrument of human rights. It recognizes any violation of the rights of people with disabilities as an infringement of human rights. It encourages governments to develop appropriate education policies and practices for these people but leaves it up to Deaf communities or their advocates to argue for what they consider to be the "most appropriate" educational policies and practices. This includes identifying the language of instruction.

The resolution also mentions deaf children's need for sign language in education, though it is put forth as a recommendation for "consideration" only: "Consideration should be given to the use of sign language in the education of deaf children, in their families and communities."

This is neither a statement of obligation nor a clear identification of the language to be used in the instruction of deaf children.

Following the introduction of the Standard Rules, in 1996 the World Federation of the Deaf (WFD) undertook a survey on government action. The subsequent report it issued identified only eleven nations (of the thirty-one national federations of deaf people who are ordinary members of the WFD) that recognized sign language as the official language of deaf people and four that reportedly used it as the first language in education. The Australian government responded to the survey by maintaining that it recognized sign language as the official language of deaf people and used it as the first language in their education. The Australian Association of the Deaf (AAD), however, reported that the Australian government had only given it official recognition. No reference was made to its use in education. A possible explanation for the inconsistency in responses comes from use of the generic term "sign language."

To the government and those unfamiliar with the existence of contrived sign systems or their difference from the native language, "sign language" may be considered an accurate descriptor for what goes on in many programs for deaf people. Indeed, with the heightened criticism of contrived systems such as Signed English, teachers now commonly describe their method of communication as "signing" or "sign language" and thereby avoid the need to identify the language they are using. Alternatively, for most deaf people, "sign language" is likely to be interpreted as their native language; hence the AAD's silence over the use of sign language in education (given the general absence of Auslan as the first language for deaf children in education).

A stronger and clearer directive is given in the Salamanca Statement on Special Needs Education (UNESCO 1994), which is a report published by the World Conference on Special Needs Education (held in Spain in 1994) that addressed the needs of students with disabilities. Item 21 called for sign language to be recognized as the medium of communication among Deaf people:

The importance of sign language as the medium of communication among the deaf, for example, should be recognized and provision made to ensure that all deaf persons have access to education in *their national sign language*. Owing to the particular communication needs of deaf and deaf/blind persons, their education may be more suitably provided in special schools or special classes and units in mainstream schools. (emphasis added)

The intended meaning of the term "sign language" is further clarified by reference to the "*national* sign language" of deaf people. The Salamanca Statement also called for action to be taken in the recruitment and training of staff with special needs to redress the general lack of role models for students with disabilities. The statement recommended that educational staff members with disabilities be recruited and successful individuals with disabilities be involved in the school program. Item 47 called for people with disabilities to be actively involved in research and training "to ensure that their perspectives are taken fully into account." Item 4 of the statement urged all governments to "encourage and facilitate the participation of parents, communities and organizations of persons with disabilities in the planning and decision-making processes concerning provision for special educational needs."

International conventions are intended to guide member states. Australia's human rights policy, for example, is based on the principle that human rights are "inherent, inalienable, indivisible and universal" (Commonwealth of Australia [CoA] 2005a, 5): "They are the birthright of all human beings, cannot be lost or taken away, are all of equal importance and apply to all persons irrespective of race, sex, disability, language, religion, political or other opinion, national or social origin, age, property or other status" (ibid.).

The 1989 *Convention on the Rights of the Child* was ratified by Australia in 1990, and although it has yet to be incorporated into Australian law, its directing influence on the courts and administrative authorities is recognized. The High Court of Australia, for example, made the following ruling:

Ratification by Australia of an International Convention is not to be dismissed as merely a platitudinous or ineffectual act, particularly when the instrument evidences internationally accepted standards to be applied by courts and administrative authorities in dealing with basic human rights affecting the family and children. Rather, ratification of a Convention is a positive statement by the Executive Government of this country to the world and to the Australian people that the Executive Government and its agencies will act in accordance with the Convention (*Minister for Immigration, Local Government, and Ethnic Affairs v. Teogh* [1995] 128 ALR 353 at [365]. (cited in Mills 2007).

Recognition of Native Sign Languages and the Protection of Linguistic Minorities

Deaf leaders of national and international organizations have appealed for self-determination and recognition of their rights as members of a cultural and linguistic minority and rejected the way in which Deaf people are characterized as deficient (Australian Association of the Deaf 1997). Since the late 1980s they have lobbied for the recognition of native sign languages and deaf children's right to bilingual education (World Federation of the Deaf 1993; UNESCO 1994). The continuing denial or marginalization of native sign languages in many nations goes against the actions requested by these organizations and the international treaties and conventions I have already mentioned.

In 1993 the WFD Scientific Commission on Sign Language published a report that recommended that native sign language be recognized and utilized as the first language of deaf children and that "teachers of the deaf must be expected to learn and use the accepted natural sign language as the primary language of instruction" (WFD 1993, 12). Ten years later, at the Fourteenth World Congress of the WFD, General Secretary Carol-Lee Aquiline reaffirmed that deaf children have a right to bilingual education in their indigenous signed and written languages. The WFD resolved to continue its work "opposing the violation of the linguistic and human right of Deaf people still common worldwide and reaffirming that Deaf children have a right to bilingual education in their indigenous sign and written languages."

.　The AAD policy on education states the following:

> Auslan is the only viable first language for Deaf people, by virtue of giving a visual understanding of the world. Therefore for effective access to education, access to Auslan is essential. A first language is vital for effective access and competence in a second language— since only a minority of Deaf people have access to Auslan as a first language from Deaf parents, first language acquisition of Auslan must be provided right through the education system. Therefore all Deaf children should have access to Auslan as a first language.
>
> Teachers should be trained to use Auslan to a level of competence before being permitted to teach Deaf children. Training programs should also include compulsory courses in Deaf Studies so that teachers can understand the cultural background of the Deaf children they teach.

Official recognition of native sign languages has been an important precursor to the shift in perception of deaf people as people with a disability to members of a linguistic minority. Deaf people and their allies have fought hard for this recognition. The British government did not grant full language status to British Sign Language (BSL) until 2003. New Zealand Sign Language did not gain official status until 2006. In turn, these successes have emboldened other Deaf communities to fight for recognition of their own languages. The degree to which those communities are protected by national legislation varies from country to country. Some nations recognize the native sign language in their constitution.

Although most Deaf people do not consider themselves to have a disability, there are political and financial reasons for accepting the disability label. Without it, they may "lose all the opportunities, benefits, and rights associated with disability" (Kauppinen 1999, 11).

However, resolutions, statements, and conventions that address the needs of people with disabilities often neglect the issue of language rights and thus offer little help to Deaf people in their struggle for bilingual education. The linguistic rights of Deaf communities may be more adequately protected by legislation and human rights instruments that address the concerns of linguistic minorities.

The discrimination that deaf people experience often has more to do with their language than their bodies, which makes them "more like oppressed language minorities than oppressed disability groups" (Lane 2005):

> Although the disability label seems inappropriate for the Deaf-World, its members have not aggressively promoted government under-standing of its ethnicity and of the poor fit of the disability label. As a result, the majority's accommodation of the Deaf has come under a disability label and Deaf people must in effect subscribe to that label in order to gain their rights in access to information, in education, and other areas. This is the Deaf dilemma: retain some important rights as members of their society at the expense of being mischaracterized by that society and government, or surrender some of those rights in the hope of gradually undermining that misconstruction.
>
> Classifying the Deaf-World as an *ethnic group* should encourage those who are concerned with Deaf people to do appropriate things: learn their language, defend their heritage against more powerful groups, study their ethnic history, and so on. In this light, the Deaf-World should enjoy the rights and protections accorded other ethnic groups under international law and treaties. (ibid.)

Recognizing the ethnic and linguistic minority status of Deaf communities would place them under the protection of the *Declaration on the Rights of Persons Belonging to National or Ethnic, Religious, and Linguistic Minorities* (General Assembly Resolution 47/135, December 18, 1992). This UN resolution recommends that states "take appropriate measures so that, wherever possible, persons belonging to minorities may have adequate opportunities to learn their mother tongue or to have instruction in their mother tongue" (Article 4[3]).

Several years later the UN General Assembly passed the *International Covenant on Civil and Political Rights* (General Assembly Resolution 2200 A [XXI], December 16, 1996), which provides for people who belong to linguistic and other minorities to have access to their native language and culture: "In those States in which ethnic, religious or linguistic minorities exist, persons belonging to such minorities shall not be denied the right, in community with other members of their group, to enjoy their own culture, to profess and practice their own religion, or to use their own language" (Article 27).

In this regard the *Hague Recommendations Regarding the Education Rights of National Minorities* (Foundation on Inter-Ethnic Relations 1996, 2) acknowledge the importance of education in preserving and deepening the identities of linguistic minorities that "can only be fully realized if they acquire a proper knowledge of their mother tongue during the educational process." Their minority language is to be used in education both as a subject and a language of instruction:

> The medium of teaching at pre-school and kindergarten levels should ideally be the child's language—the curriculum should ideally be taught in the minority language. The minority language should be taught as a subject on a regular basis. The official State language should also be taught as a subject on a regular basis preferably by bilingual teachers who have a good understanding of the children's cultural and linguistic background. (ibid., 3)

Given these and other international conventions, it is both reasonable and fair to expect teachers who are otherwise qualified to work in a specialist field to adopt the language of the linguistic minority they serve.

These ideals have been articulated by Deaf leaders and bilingual educators who call for Auslan (or the native sign languages of other countries) to be used as the first language and language of instruction and for the majority language to be taught as a second language, largely through reading and writing. At the national level, a transition from the disability construction of deafness would open the way for deaf people to make claims on legislation that provides support and resources to the members of other ethnic groups. In the United States, for example, the Civil Rights Act, the Equal Educational Opportunities Act, and the Bilingual Education Act could all be cited in support of bilingual education for deaf children. The right of linguistic minorities in Australia to use their language in community with others is similarly protected. However, the right to access that language in education has not been made explicit: "In those States in which ethnic, religious or linguistic minorities exist, persons belonging to such minorities shall not be denied the right, in community with the other members of their group, to enjoy their own culture, to profess and practice their own religion, or to use their own language (Ruddock 2004, 81).

Australia has recognized the legitimacy of Auslan as a community language (Lo Bianco 1987) and the Deaf community as a cultural and linguistic minority in government policy (Department of Employment, Education, and Training 1991). Although the inclusion of Auslan in *Australia's Language: The Australian Language and Literacy Policy* was a significant development, the document backed away from the issue of using native sign language in education. It claimed that using Auslan as the method of instruction was controversial because most deaf children come from English-speaking families. It called for deaf people to have complete access to a first language but did not name that language. The policy recommended that educational systems consider the benefits of teaching Auslan to both deaf and hearing students.

In Sweden, legislative action brought about changes to language policy when Parliament endorsed the goal of bilingualism for deaf people in 1981. The law recognized Swedish Sign Language as the first language of deaf children as a result of the activism of the National Federation of the Deaf, the Association of Parents of Deaf Children, and linguists at the University of Stockholm. It declared that for "the profoundly deaf to function among themselves and in society [they] have to be bilingual. Bilingualism . . . means that they have to be fluent in their visual/gestural Sign Language and be fluent in the language that society surrounds them with: Swedish" (Bergman 1990, 176).

In 1983 the development of bilingualism as an educational goal for deaf children was written into a supplement of the national curriculum. In 1995 a new curriculum strengthened the requirement that deaf students be bilingual by the time they left school and required schools to provide the equivalent of a regular school curriculum (Svartholm 1995). This forced further change because "teachers were put in a situation where the curriculum, the parents and the pupils (and the deaf association) demanded a proficiency in sign language that the traditional teacher training never offered them" (Ahlgren 1990, 91).

Similarly, in 1992 the Danish Ministry of Education ordered that Danish Sign Language be taught in all public schools and classes for deaf students; Norwegian Sign Language is recognized by law for use in compulsory schooling; and Finnish Sign Language is protected by law and recognized in the national school curriculum as deaf children's mother tongue (Jokinen 1999).

CHAPTER 7

Conclusion

B ECAUSE LANGUAGE EXISTS WITHIN a sociocultural context, it is therefore political and bound up with issues of power. For linguistic
minorities, the concern is not only *how* language is used in education but
also *which* language is used in the classroom. Schools are powerful institutions whose language practices maintain or challenge the positions of
particular cultural and linguistic groups. Change requires educators to
reconsider the assumptions that underlie their practices. Deaf education
has long been an example of cultural imperialism, in which deaf children
have been "defined from the outside, positioned, and placed by a system
of dominant meanings . . . arising from elsewhere, from those with
whom they do not identify and who do not identify with them" (Young
1992, 192).

Are educators directly manipulating language practices to achieve political goals (see Nover 1995)? Are they denying deafness and illegitimating
the Deaf identity (see Bouvet 1990)? Or are educators well intentioned?
The practices that dominate education and thus become established are
the result, rather than the intention, of educators' actions (Lankshear
1997). The deeds of many well-intentioned individuals, though not
overtly discriminatory, keep oppression alive (Young 1992). Educators
who almost exclusively come from the dominant group perpetuate the
power and status relationships within the wider society. Teachers of deaf

children have a professional responsibility to reflect on their practices and consider the criticism from Deaf people, researchers, and other educators.

Systems do not usually change at the top, and new skills, understanding, and commitment cannot be mandated. Rather, "it is the cumulative actions of individuals, connected together, which make change" (Fullan 1993, 4). However, it is necessary to consider the political factors that block advancements in deaf education and determine how to effect change in the wider profession. Until now, bilingual deaf education in Australia has resulted from the actions of individuals, not from the decisions of policymakers at the state or national level. Teachers of deaf students who believe in bilingual education have remained at the center of the reform process, a positive approach to educational development. There is a risk, however, that individual teachers, teacher educators, or policymakers who oppose the bilingual approach may obstruct that change.

A central aim of this book has been to provide a powerful and realistic account of the political barriers and social injustices Deaf people face every day. Deaf education is charged with paternalism and hearing ethnocentrism, and this situation will not be remedied until Deaf people have positions of influence in deaf education and Auslan is accepted as deaf students' primary language. Deaf education should ensure that deaf children leave school fluent in the language of the Deaf community and literate in the language of the wider society. Educators must consider a perspective that is outside their own hearing purview.

The changes that are needed in educational policy, practice, and teacher education can be made, but they require radical shifts in language policy and educational practices. Auslan use is restricted today, directly and indirectly, due to the paucity of Deaf teachers employed or qualified to teach deaf children, the policy of using English as the main or only language of instruction, and the lack of hearing teachers who are competent in Auslan.

Schools that have adopted bilingual education and teachers who have acquired Auslan have overcome the structural and personal barriers to change. They have challenged the view that deaf children have difficulty acquiring language or succeeding in education. They have confronted their own language practices. They have worked with the parents in their school communities or arranged for someone with the skills to do so to provide information on Auslan and bilingual education.

The adoption of bilingual education directly challenges the practices of most teachers of deaf children, previous language policies, and teacher education philosophies. Therefore, support from the most-experienced teachers is essential in bringing about changes. Teachers need significant backing and encouragement if they are to be willing to consider adopting a new language for classroom instruction. Most have not had access to information on Auslan and bilingual education and will need ongoing in-service education to enable them to acquire Auslan. They need to be exposed to the normal linguistic development of Deaf children from Deaf families and to a model of Auslan use in education.

Educational authorities in Australia must formally endorse bilingual education and establish it in government schools. Given the dissatisfaction with existing practices (in particular oral education and the use of Signed English in Total Communication [TC] settings), the establishment of bilingual education is justified. The general failure of deaf students in education can no longer be explained by their deafness, lack of communication in the home, or learning difficulties or disabilities. Given the continued underachievement of deaf students, it is time for teachers to examine their methods. Criticism of these methods is widespread in the literature and among Deaf leaders and bilingual educators, yet many educators in Australia, like their American counterparts (see Hoffmeister 1996) have failed to modify their methods.

Adopting bilingual education will require schools to review their educational practices, focus on changing teachers' beliefs and attitudes, and develop teachers' skills in Auslan and bilingual pedagogy. Teachers of deaf children require information on current research and professional discussion in deaf education on first- and second-language learning theory, bilingual pedagogy, and the efficacy of established practices. I have found that educators who continue to endorse oral education or TC practices are generally unfamiliar with the literature that supports native sign language. They remain unaware of—or dismiss—the poor results of simultaneous communication, as well as the documented inadequacy of Signed English and its inaccuracy as a model of English (see Leigh 1995).

These teachers continue to use Signed English because they believe that it will enable deaf children to acquire language and literacy. Teachers who instruct in English persist in citing learning difficulties, disabilities, or lack of communication in the home as the reasons for their students' underachievement. Some teachers are unmoved by criticism of their methods by other educators and Deaf adults, and they see no need to investigate alternative techniques. Some view Auslan as unnecessary for their students or inappropriate for the educational setting. And some do not understand the philosophy behind bilingual education or how Auslan can be used to teach literacy.

Australia urgently needs more Deaf teachers of deaf children. This will require federal and state departments of education to establish affirmative action policies and programs to recruit and qualify Deaf adults as TODs and parent advisers. Viewing deaf students as minority language bilinguals requires schools to provide access to positive Auslan-using Deaf role models. State departments of education can no longer justify their lack of involvement in issues of language and communication practices in schools for deaf children. Managers within these departments must seriously consider establishing bilingual education as a viable option in deaf education. Introducing Auslan as a language-other-than-English subject fails to address the issue of deaf students' disadvantage when faced with monolingual teaching practices. The language policies of schools for deaf children have discouraged teachers' use of Auslan and left some TODs feeling isolated and powerless to change their school's approach, while educators are unlikely to initiate changes without support from their colleagues and the parents.

Parents need information and guidance from Deaf adults and hearing professionals who are fluent in Auslan and knowledgeable about bilingual education. Parents' desire for their children to acquire spoken and written English should not be viewed as endorsement of monolingual practices. For many years, parents have been told that deafness is a disability and is the reason their child fails to attain age-appropriate language and literacy development. These same parents were not given an opportunity to learn Auslan or to consider its benefit to their children's education. Once informed, many are eager to adopt a bilingual approach to their child's education.

A policy of affirmative action may encourage Deaf adults to enter teacher education and raise the employment numbers of Deaf teachers in Australia from its present level of 2.6 percent and to increase the number of culturally and linguistically Deaf TODs from its present level of 0.9 percent. More flexible training requirements are also needed in order to qualify Deaf adults as teachers. For example, the approach to teacher education in Sweden is to provide deaf people with the choice of attending regular classes with the support of interpreters or classes conducted in Swedish Sign Language. In Australia this approach may better meet the needs of Deaf adults who are native Auslan users.

Hearing teachers of deaf students must be required to be proficient users of Auslan in order to obtain certification. I contend that, without fluency, teachers cannot provide accessible pedagogy to deaf students. Lack of Auslan skills is a major barrier to introducing bilingual education in Australia. This proposition is consistent with the view of the World Federation of the Deaf (WFD) Scientific Commission on Sign Language, which recommended that "teachers of the deaf must be expected to learn and use the accepted natural sign language as the primary language of instruction" (WFD 1993, 12). The commission called for native sign language to be included in programs that educate teachers of deaf children.

Departments of education need to establish extensive professional development programs to enable TODs who are currently employed in deaf education to acquire Auslan and become versed in the methods of bilingual pedagogy. Proficiency in Auslan should become a requirement for all teachers of deaf students, including those currently employed by government and private authorities. The present lack of instruction in Auslan in the preservice education of TODs places responsibility on the schools to provide a comprehensive program of professional development. In Victoria this is largely the obligation of individual schools. Funds for professional training have been located within schools, and decisions on priorities and spending can now be made at the local level.

Educators who want to pursue bilingual education need to secure support within the school. They may be unable to do so, however, without a commitment to new practices from senior TODs. There is a risk that professional development activities will exclude instruction in Auslan and thereby maintain the status quo and reflect these teachers' traditional beliefs. Even with a high level of commitment to changes in language policy and practices, it may be unrealistic to expect schools to provide the level of training necessary for teachers of deaf children to become fluent in Auslan without support from state authorities. Between 1996 and 1997 the South Australian Department of Education provided time-release scholarships to six teachers to enable them to become fluent in Auslan (L. MacKenzie, personal communication, July 3, 1997). Teachers of deaf students who are already employed in deaf education should not be expected to acquire Auslan on their own time or at their own expense, which is the present situation for many teachers. Moreover, deaf children should not be left in classrooms without access to fluent language models.

Another important factor in providing deaf students with accessible pedagogy is the presence of Deaf adults in the classroom. Are hearing professionals willing to establish affirmative action policies in their schools that will give *preference* to hiring Deaf staff? What effort will they make to raise the number of qualified culturally and linguistically Deaf TODs in Australia from the current level of 0.9 percent to, say, 50 percent or greater? Will Deaf adults who are currently unqualified or underqualified be recruited, financially supported, and encouraged to become qualified teachers? Will the complaints that Deaf leaders make about the paternalism of hearing educators and the necessity for Deaf teachers go unheeded? Choice in deaf education can truly exist only when we have significant numbers of Deaf teachers and hearing staff who are skilled in Auslan.

Connection to the Deaf World and awareness of its members' identity empowers Deaf people to meet the challenges of living in a hearing world. The denial of linguistic and cultural differences between deaf and hearing children ignores the situation in which deaf children find themselves. To effect change, educators must become aware of the discriminatory practices within their own schools (Edelsky 1991). Language practices in deaf education should recognize the needs of deaf children as minority language bilinguals. Before significant changes in deaf education can come about, educators will have to recognize the disadvantage imposed on deaf students by a system of education dominated by hearing teachers who are unable to instruct these students in their own language. If the system cannot be changed from within, legislation will ultimately be needed to ensure that deaf children's linguistic rights are upheld.

References

Agostino, M. 1999. Development of Disability Standards in Education. Paper presented at the Human Rights, Disability and Education Conference, September, Sydney.

Ahlgren, I. 1990. Swedish Conditions: Sign Language in Deaf Education. In *Sign Language Research and Application. Proceedings of the International Congress on Sign Language Research and Application*, ed. S. Prillwitz and T. Wollhaber. International Studies on Sign Language and Communication of the Deaf, vol. 13, Hamburg: Signum-Press.

Ahlgren, I., and K. Hyltenstam, eds. 1994. *Bilingualism in Deaf Education: Proceedings of the International Conference on Bilingualism in Deaf Education, Stockholm, Sweden*. International Studies on Sign Language and Communication of the Deaf, 27.

Andersson, Y. 1990. Who Should Make Decisions on Communication among Deaf People? In *Eyes, Hands, Voices: Communication Issues among Deaf People: A Deaf American Monograph*, ed. M. D. Garretson, vol. 40, 1–4. Silver Spring, Md.: National Association of the Deaf.

Australian Association of the Deaf. 1997. Australian Association of the Deaf: Auslan Policy. Unpublished policy.

Australian Association of Teachers of the Deaf. 2005. Competencies for Teachers of the Deaf, Endorsed by the AATD National Committee. Unpublished report, March 17.

Bacchi, C. 1996. *The Politics of Affirmative Action*. London: Sage.

Bacchi, C., and J. Eveline. 1996. The Politics of Incorporation. In *Affirmative Action in Context: Category Politics and the Case for 'Women,'* ed. C. Bacchi, London: Sage.

Ball, S. J. 1993. Education, Majorism and the Curriculum of the Dead. *Curriculum Studies* 1 (2): 195–214.

Bergmann, R. 1994. Teaching Sign Language as a Mother Tongue in the Education of Deaf Children in Denmark. In *Biligualism in Deaf Education*, ed. I. Ahlgren and I. K. Hyltenstam, 83–90. Hamburg: Signum.

Boutros-Ghali, Boutros. 1995. Address to the XII World Congress of the World Federation of the Deaf, Vienna.

Bouvet, D. 1990. *The Path to Language: Bilingual Education for Deaf Children.* Philadelphia: Multilingual Matters.

Branson, J., and D. Miller. 1989. Beyond Integration Policy: The Deconstruction of Disability. In *Integration: Myth or Reality?* ed. Len Barton. London: Farmer.

———. 1993. Sign Language, the Deaf, and the Epistemic Violence of Mainstreaming. *Language and Education* 7 (1): 21–41.

———. 1991. Language and Identity in the Australian Deaf Community: Australian Sign Language and Language Policy, an Issue of Social Justice. *Australian Review of Applied Linguistics*, series S, 8: 135–76.

Burch, E., and M. Hyde. 1984. Deaf Adults and Total Communication: A Questionnaire Survey of Knowledge, Attitudes, and Use. *Australian Teacher of the Deaf* 25: 34–38.

Butler, J. 1992. Contingent Foundations: Feminism and the Question of Postmodernism. In *Feminists Theorize the Political*, ed. Judith Butler and Joan Scott, 3–21. London: Routledge.

Cambourne, B. 1990. Beyond the Deficit Theory: A 1990s' Perspective on Literacy Failure. *Australian Journal of Reading* 13(4): 289–99.

Cambourne, B., and H. Brown. 1987. A Grounded Theory of Genre Acquisition: Learning to Control Different Textual Forms. *Australian Journal of Reading* 10(4): 261–66.

Carty, B. 1994. The Australian Association of the Deaf and Its "Parents." *AAD Outlook* 4(2): 8–14.

Cherryholmes, C. H. 1988. *Power and Criticism: Poststructural Investigations in Education.* New York: Teachers College Press.

Cicourel, A. V., and R. J. Boese. 1972a. Sign Language Acquisition and the Teaching of Deaf Children, Part I. *American Annals of the Deaf* 117(1): 27–33.

———. 1972b. Sign Language Acquisition and the Teaching of Deaf Children Part II. *American Annals of the Deaf*, 117(3): 403–411.

Clark, G. 2000. *Sounds from Silence: Graeme Clark and the Bionic Ear Story.* St. Leonards, New South Wales: Allen and Unwin.

Cohen, O. P. Introduction. In *Implications and Complications for Deaf Students of the Full Inclusion Moment*, ed. R. Johnson and O. Cohen, 1–6. Washington, D.C.: Gallaudet University Press.

Cohen, D., M. McLaughlin, and J. Talbert. 1993. *Teaching for Understanding: Challenges for Policy and Practice.* San Francisco: Jossey Bass.

Coleman, B., J. Walsh, A. Pavia, S. Leane, and M. Bartlett. 2000. A Bilingual/Bicultural Early Educational Program in a Victorian Government

School. Paper presented at the 19th International Congress on Education of the Deaf and 7th Asia-Pacific Congress on Deafness, July 9–13, Sydney.

Commonwealth of Australia. 1992. *Disability Discrimination Act 1992*. Canberra: Australian Government Printer.

———. 2005a. Australia's National Framework for Human Rights: National Action Plan. Canberra, Commonwealth of Australia. http://www.ag.gov.au/agd/WWW/civiljusticeHome.nsf/0/0F9F219C19427392CA256F6C00150967?OpenDocument (accessed March 13, 2007).

———. 2005b. Disability Standards for Education 2005. http://www.dest.gov.au/NR/rdonlyres/482C1E4B-9848-4CC3-B395-067D79853095/4592/Disability_Standards_for_Education_2005.pdf (accessed November 10, 2005).

Crickmore, B. 1995. *Education of the Deaf and Hearing Impaired: A Brief History*. 2d. ed. Mayfield, Australia: Education Management Systems.

Crittenden, J. B. 1993. The Culture and Identity of Deafness. In *Toward a Psychology of Deafness: Theoretical and Empirical Perspectives*, ed. P. V. Paul and D. W. Jackson, 215–35. Needham Heights, Mass.: Allyn and Bacon.

Cummins, J. 1986. Empowering Minority Students: A Framework for Intervention. *Harvard Educational Review* 56(1): 18–36.

———. 1989. A Theoretical Framework for Bilingual Special Education. *Exceptional Children*, 56(2): 111–19.

Davies, S. 1991a. Deaf Children's Acquisition of Sign Language as a First Language: Swedish Views. *Bicultural Centre News* 33:4–6.

———. 1991b. The Transition toward Bilingual Education of Deaf Children in Sweden and Denmark: Perspectives on Language. *Sign Language Studies* 17: 169–94.

———. 1994. Attributes for Success: Attitudes and Practices that Facilitate the Transition toward Bilingualism in the Education of Deaf Children. In *Bilingualism in Deaf Education: Proceedings of the International Conference on Bilingualism in Deaf Education, Stockholm, Sweden*, ed. I. Ahlgren and K. Hyltenstam, 10321. Hamburg: Signum.

De Groof, J., and G. Lauwers. 2002. Education Policy and Law: The Politics of Multiculturalism in Education. *Education and the Law* 14(1–2): 7–23.

Department of Education and the Arts. 2002. CS-11: Total Communication for Deaf/Hearing Impaired. Queensland Government. http://education.qld.gov.au/corporate/doem/curristu/cs-11000/sections/procedur.html (accessed March 13, 2007).

Department of Education, Employment and Training. 1991. *Australia's Language: The Australian Language and Literacy Policy.* Canberra: Australian Government Publishing Service.

Drasgow, E. 1993. Bilingual/Bicultural Deaf Education: An Overview. *Sign Language Studies,* 80: 243–65.

Edelsky, C. 1991. *With Literacy and Justice for All: Rethinking the Social in Language and Education.* Critical Perspectives on Literacy and Education. London: Falmer.

Erting, C. 1992. Deafness and Literacy: Why Can't Sam Read? *Sign Language Studies* 75: 97–112.

Ewing, I. R., and A. W. G Ewing. 1938. *The Handicap of Deafness.* London: Longmans.

———. 1950. General Report to the Commonwealth Office of Education. Unpublished report.

Fine, M. 1994. Distance and Other Stances: Negotiations of Power Inside Feminist Research. In *Power and Method: Political Activism and Educational Research,* ed. A. Gitlin, 13–35. London: Routledge.

Foster, V. 1992. Different but Equal? Dilemmas in the Reform of Girls' Education. *Australian Journal of Education* 36(1): 53–67.

Foundation on Inter-Ethnic Relations. 1996. *Hague Recommendations Regarding the Education Rights of National Minorities.* The Hague: Author.

Fraser, N. 1997. *Justice Interruptus.* New York: Routledge.

Friedlander, J. 1993. Letter to Disability Discrimination Commissioner. *Sound News* 21 (4): 8.

Gifford, F. 1997. January. Bilingualism and Integration: The Claremont Project. Paper presented at the Australian and New Zealand Conference for Educators of the Deaf, 8–11, Adelaide, Australia.

Gilbert, P. 1993. (Sub)versions: Using Sexist Language Practices to Explore Critical Literacy. *Australian Journal of Language and Literacy* 16(4): 323–31.

Giroux, H. A. 1992. *Border Crossings: Cultural Workers and the Politics of Education.* New York: Routledge.

Gitlin, A., ed. 1994. *Power and Method: Political Activism and Educational Research.* New York: Routledge.

Gitlin, A., M. Siegel, and K. Boru. 1993. The Politics of Method: From Leftist Ethnography to Educative Research. In *Educational Research: Current Issues* Vol. 1, ed. M. Hammersely, 191–210. London: Open University.

Graham, B. 1994. A System Approach to the Issue of Bilingual/Bicultural Education of Deaf Children. *The Australian Teacher of the Deaf* 34: 61–63.

Grosjean, F. 1992. The Bilingual and the Bicultural Person in the Hearing and in the Deaf World. *Sign Language Studies* 77: 307–20.

———. 1996. Living with Two Languages and Two Cultures. In *Cultural and Language Diversity and the Deaf Experience*, ed. I. Parsnis, 20–37. New York: Cambridge University Press.

Hansen, B. 1990. Trends in the Progress towards Bilingual Education for Deaf Children in Denmark. In *Sign Language Research and Application: Proceedings of the International Congress*, ed. S. Prillwitz and T. Vollhaber, vol. 13, 51–62. Hamburg: Signum Press.

Hastings, E. 1997. The Right to Belong: Disability Discrimination Law in Education. Speech by the Disability Discrimination Commissioner, Sydney, July 1997, http://www.hreoc.gov.au/disability_rights/speeches/1997/edspeech.html (accessed May 10, 2007).

Heiling, K. 1995. *The Development of Deaf Children: Academic Achievement Levels and Social Process*. Hamburg: Signum.

Held, D. 1991. Introduction. In *Political Theory Today*, ed. D. Held, 1–22. Stanford: Stanford University Press.

Henshaw, L. 2003. Special Education Needs and the Law: Some Practical Implications. *Education and the Law* 15(1): 3–18.

Hoffmeister, R. J. 1996. Cross-Cultural Misinformation: What Does Special Education Say about Deaf People. *Disability and Society* 11(2): 171–89.

Howe, B. 1992. The Second Reading of the Disability Discrimination Act 1992 by the Honourable Brian Howe, Minister for Health, Housing, and Community Services to Federal Parliament on May 26, 1992. http://www.hreoc.gov.au/disability_rights/legislation/reps2r1.htm (accessed March 10, 2007).

Human Rights and Equal Opportunity Commission. 2000. *Debbie Murphy vs. State of New South Wales*, http://www.hreoc.gov.au/disability_rights/decisions/comdec/2000/DD000090.htm (accessed May 10, 2007).

———. 2000. Decline/Termination Decisions: Education, http://www.hreoc.gov.au/disability_rights/decisions/decline/decline_education.html (accessed May 10, 2007).

———. 2002. Conciliation Register for Complaints Conciliated and Finalized between April 1, 2002, and June 30, 2002. http://www.humanrights.gov.au/complaints_information/register/dda/pdf/dda-apr_june.pdf (accessed May 10, 2007).

————. 2005a. Human Rights and Equal Opportunity Commission. Complaints Information: Conciliation Register, http://www.hreoc.gov.au/complaints_information/register/index.html (accessed May 10, 2007) (updated quarterly).

————. 2005b. Conciliated Outcomes: Education. Available at http://www.hreoc.gov.au/disability_rights/decisions/conciliation/education_conciliation.html (accessed May 10, 2007).

Hyde, M. B., and D. J. Power. 1991. Teachers' Use of Simultaneous Communication: Effects on the Signed and Spoken Components. *American Annals of the Deaf* 136(5): 381–87.

————. 1992. The Use of Australian Sign Language by Deaf People. *Sign Language Studies* 75: 167–82.

Hyde, M., and S. Cliffe. 1992. Teachers' Communication with Their Deaf Students: An Australian Study. *Sign Language Studies* 75: 159–66.

Iskov, Q. 1994. But Is It Cricket? Signed English at Marion High School. *AAD Outlook* 4 (4): 18–19.

Israelite, N., C. Ewoldt, and R. Hoffmeister. 1992. *Bilingual/Bicultural Education for Deaf and Hard of Hearing Students: A Review of the Literature on the Effects of Native Sign Language on Majority Language Acquisition*. Ontario, Canada: Ministry of Education.

Jankowski, K. 1995. Empowerment from Within: The Deaf Social Movement Providing a Framework for a Multicultural Society. In *Sociolinguistics in Deaf Communities*, ed. C. Lucas, 307–29. Washington, D.C.: Gallaudet University Press.

Jeanes, D. R. 1970. Language Development under the Combined Method. *Australian Teacher of the Deaf*, 11(1): 42–47.

Jeanes, R., and B. E. Reynolds, eds. 1982. *Dictionary of Australasian Signs for Communication with the Deaf*. Melbourne: Victorian School for the Deaf Children.

Jenkinson, J. C. 1997. *Mainstream or Special? Educating Students with Disabilities*. New York: Routledge.

Johnson, N. J. 1993. A Celebration of Teaching and Teachers as Learners. Paper presented at The Australian College of Education National Conference: Global Curriculum, September 28–October 1, Melbourne.

Johnson, R. E., S. K. Liddell, and C. J. Erting. 1989. "Unlocking the Curriculum: Principles for Achieving Access in Deaf Education." Washington, D.C: Gallaudet University Research Institute.

Johnston, T. 1989. *Auslan Dictionary: A Dictionary of the Sign Language for the Australian Deaf Community*. Sydney: Deafness Resources Australia.

Jokinen, M. 1999. New Teacher Education Programme of Finnish Sign Language Users—Training Students to Become Qualifying Teachers to Work with Finnish Sign Language Using Pupils in Comprehensive School in Finland. In *Proceedings of EDDE 99, Bilingual Education with a Focus on Reading and Writing, September 23–26, 1999*. Örebro.

Kannapell, B. 1990. Personal Reflections: Current Issues on Language and Communication among Deaf People. In *Eyes, Hands, Voices: Communication Issues among Deaf People*, vol. 40, *A Deaf American Monograph*, ed. M. D. Garretson, 65–69. Silver Spring, Md.: National Association of the Deaf.

Kauppinen, L. 1999. Are Deaf People Disabled? *WFD News* (July).

Komesaroff, L. 1998. The Politics of Language Practices in Deaf Education. PhD diss., Deakin University, Geelong, Australia.

———. 2005. The Case for Signing: The Way in Which Auslan Is Viewed in Recent Legal Cases in the Federal Court of Australia. Paper presented at the International Congress for Educators of the Deaf, July 17–20, Maastricht, the Netherlands.

———, ed. 2007. *Surgical Consent: Bioethics and Cochlear Implantation*. Washington, D.C.: Gallaudet University Press.

Ladd, P. 2003. *Understanding Deaf Culture: In Search of Deafhood*. London: Multilingual Matters.

Lane, H. 1984. *When the Mind Hears: A History of the Deaf*. New York: Random House.

———. 1996. Deaf-Centered Education and Empowerment. Paper presented at the National Deafness Conference, Hobart, Tasmania, Australia, May 22–26.

———. 2003 Fighting for Linguistic Rights 'Down Under': Bringing Australian Schools and Departments of Education to Account. *14th World Congress of the World Federation of the Deaf*, 1–13. World Federation of the Deaf, Canada

———. 2005. Ethnicity, Ethics, and the Deaf World. *Journal of Deaf Studies and Deaf Education* 10 (3): 291–310.

———. 2007. Ethnicity, Ethics, and the Deaf World. In *Surgical Consent: Bioethics and Cochlear Implantation*, ed. L. Komesaroff, 42–69. Washington, D.C.: Gallaudet University Press.

H. Lane, R. Hoffmeister, and B. Bahan. 1996. *A Journey into the DEAF-WORLD*. San Diego: DawnSignPress.

Lankshear, C. 1997. *Changing Literacies*. Buckingham: Open University Press.

Lather, P. 1991. *Getting Smart: Feminist Research and Pedagogy with/in the Postmodern.* New York: Routledge.

Leigh, G. R. 1995. Teachers' Use of Australasian Signed English System for Simultaneous Communication with Their Hearing-Impaired Students. PhD diss., Monash University, Melbourne.

Lewis, K. 2001. Pluralism in the Australian Print Media. *AsiaPacific Media-Educator,* 11 (July–December): 100–112.

Lloyd, K. 2001. The DDA as a Tool for Change: The Australian Association of the Deaf Point of View. Paper presented at the HREOC Summit. Retrieved October 9, 2003, from http://www.aad.org.au/download .dda.pdf.

Lo Bianco, J. 1987. *National Policy on Languages.* Canberra: Australian Government Publishing Service.

MacDougall, J. C. 1988. The Development of the Australasian Signed English System. *Australian Teacher of the Deaf* 29:18–36.

Mahshie, S. N. 1995. *Educating Deaf Children Bilingually.* Washington, D.C.: Gallaudet University.

Malzkuhn, M., J. Covell, G. Hlibok, and B. Bourne-Firl. 1994. Deaf President Now. In *The Deaf Way: Perspectives from the International Conference on Deaf Culture,* ed. C. J. Erting, R. C. Johnson, D. L. Smith, and B. D. Snider, 829–37. Washington, D.C.: Gallaudet University Press.

Mayer, P., and S. Lowenbraun. 1990. Total Communication Use among Elementary Teachers of Hearing-Impaired Children. *American Annals of the Deaf,* 135(3): 257–63.

Mills, E. Parents, Children, and Medical Treatment: Legal Rights and Responsibilities. In *Surgical Consent: Bioethics and Cochlear Implantation,* ed. Linda Komesaroff, 70–87. Washington, D.C.: Gallaudet University Press.

Moore, T. 1997. Sign Language and Signing Systems: The Choices Facing Parents and Educators. *Monnington Magazine* (Summer): 3–7.

Munshi, D., and D. McKie. 2001. Different Bodies of Knowledge: Diversity and Diversification in Public Relations, *Australian Journal of Communication,* 28 (3): 11–22.

Murdoch, K., and N. Johnson. 1994. The Role of the Outsider in School and Classroom Improvement and Change. Paper presented at the International Congress for School Effectiveness and Improvement: Quality, Equality and the Outcomes of Schooling: Imperatives for Global Development, January 3–6, Melbourne.

North, J. 1993. Rationale and Overview of the Bilingual/Bicultural Program at the Royal NSW Institute for Deaf and Blind Children. Paper presented at the Seminar on Bilingual Education for Deaf Children, November 13, Melbourne.

Nover, S. M. 1995. Politics and Language: American Sign Language and English in Deaf Education. In *Sociolinguistics in Deaf Communities*, ed. C. Lucas, 109–63. Washington, D.C.: Gallaudet University Press.

Nunan, T., G. Rigmor, and H. McCausland. 2000. Inclusive Education in Universities: Why It Is Important and How It Might Be Achieved. *International Journal of Inclusive Education* 4 (1): 63–88

Oakley, A. 1981. Interviewing Women: A Contradiction in Terms. In *Doing Feminist Research*, ed. H. Roberts, 33–61. London: Routledge and Kegan Paul.

Padden, C. A. 1996. From the Cultural to the Bicultural: The Modern Deaf Community. In *Cultural and Language Diversity and the Deaf Experience*, ed. I. Parasnis, 79–98. New York: Cambridge University Press.

———, and T. Humphries. 1988. *Deaf in America: Voices from a Culture.* Cambridge, Mass.: Harvard University Press.

Parent Council for Deaf Education. 1996. Letters of Response Re Disability Discrimination Action. *Sound News* 24(1): 21–32.

———. 1998. Disability Discrimination Action between Parent Council for Deaf Education and the Department of School Education. *Sound News* 26(1): 5.

Paterson, J., and K. O'Reilly. 1997. Bilingualism: Where Have We Come From, Where Are We Going? Paper presented at the Australian and New Zealand Conference for Educators of the Deaf, January 8–11, Adelaide, Australia.

Power, D. 1975. *Hearing-Impaired School Leavers in Victoria, 1974*, Papers in Special Education, no. 2. Burwood, Victoria, Melbourne, Australia: Burwood State College.

———. 1994. Deaf and Hard-of-Hearing Children. In *Educating Children with Special Needs*, ed. A. Ashman and J. Elkins. Sydney, Australia: Prentice Hall.

———. 1996a. Auslan *Is* a Language. *Australian Language Matters* 4(4): 12.

———. 1996b. *Language, Culture, and Community: Deaf People and Sign Language in Australia.* Centre for Deafness Studies and Research Occasional Paper no. 25. Queensland: Griffith University Press.

Pringle, R., and S. Watson. 1992. "Women's Interests" and the Poststructuralist State. In *Destabilising Theory: Contemporary Feminist Debates*, ed. M. Barrett and A. Phillips, Cambridge: Polity Press.

Reagan, T. 1995. Neither Easy to Understand Nor Pleasing to See: The Development of Manual Sign Codes as Language Planning Activity. *Language Problems and Language Planning*, 19(2): 133–50.

Richards, J. 1997. Developing a Bilingual/Bicultural Program as a Further Education Option in Western Australia. Paper presented at Australian and New Zealand Conference for Educators of the Deaf, January 8–11, Adelaide, Australia.

Richards, T., and L. Richards. 1991. The NUDIST Qualitative Data Analysis System. *Qualitative Sociology* 14.

Rizvi, F., and B. Lingard. 1996. Disability, Education, and the Discourses of Justice. In *Disability and the Dilemmas of Education and Justice*, ed. C. Christensen and F. Rizvi, 9–26. Philadelphia: Open University Press.

Rodda, M., C. Cumming, and D. Fewer. 1993. Memory, Learning, and Language: Implications for Deaf Education. In *Psychological Perspectives on Deafness*, ed. M. Marschark and M. D. Clark, 339–51. Mahwah, N.J.: Erlbaum.

Ruddock, P. 2004. Towards a Less Litigious Australia: The Australian Government's Alternative Dispute Resolution Initiatives. http://www.ag.gov .au/agd/www/Agdhome.nsf/Page/RWPC869D2824DC653D8CA2 56E98002268CE?OpenDocument#fn13 (accessed November 9, 2005).

Skutnabb-Kangas, T., and R. Phillipson. 1994. Linguistic Human Rights, Past and Present. In *Linguistic Human Rights: Overcoming Linguistic Discrimination*, ed. T. Skutnabb-Kangas and R. Phillipson, 1–110. New York: Mouton de Gruyter.

Stevens, K., K. Smitt, G. Thomas, and L. Wilson. 1995. Recording and Evaluation of Students' Use of Auslan (Australian Sign Language) to Investigate the Effectiveness of a Bilingual Approach to the Education of Deaf Students. *Australian Journal of Education of the Deaf* 1 (1): 10–14.

Stokoe, W. C. 1960. *Sign Language Structure: An Outline of the Visual Communication System of the American Deaf*. Studies in Linguistics, Occasional Paper 8. Buffalo, N.Y.: University of Buffalo.

Svartholm, K. 1993. Bilingual Education for the Deaf in Sweden. *Sign Language Studies* 81: 291–332.

———. 1994. Second Language Learning in the Deaf. In *Bilingualism in Deaf Education: Proceedings of the International Conference on Bilingualism in Deaf Education, Stockholm, Sweden*, ed. I. Ahlgren and K. Hyltenstam.

International Studies on Sign Language and Communication of the Deaf. Vol. 27. Hamburg, Germany: Signum Press.

————. 1995. Bilingual Education for the Deaf: Evaluation of the Swedish Model. In *Proceedings of the XII World Congress of the World Federation, Towards Human Rights, Vienna, 6–15 July*, 413–17.

Tarra, G. 1880. Cenni storici e compendiosa esposizione del metodo seguito per l'istruzione dei sordo-muti poveri d'ambo i sessi della Provincia e Diocesi di Milano . . . Milan: Tipografia di S. Giuseppe.

Toohey, K., and H. Hurwitz. 2002. Alternative Dispute Resolution in Education: Case Studies in Resolving Complaints of Disability Discrimination. Paper presented at the 2002 National Mediation Conference, Canberra, September 18–20, http://www.hreoc.gov.au/complaints_ information/publications/alternative_edu.html#endnote1.

Uebergang, K. 2005. Deaf Child in $50,000 Compo Bid. *Herald-Sun* (June 1), p. 13.

UNESCO. 1994. Salamanca Statement on Special Needs Education. Paris: Author.

————. 2004. *Daniels v The Attorney-General*: Children with Special Needs and the Right to Education in New Zealand. *International Journal of Education Law and Policy* (World Conference edition), 1 (1–2): 300–5.

United Nations. 1989. Implementation of the World Programme of Action Concerning Disabled Persons and the United Nations Decade of Disabled Persons (78th Plenary Meeting Resolution 44/70), gopher.un .org/00/ga/recs/44/70.

Varnham, S. 2003. Who's to Blame? May a School be Liable for the Intentional Torts of Their Employees? *Education and the Law* 15(2/3): 183–200.

————. 2004. Physical, Emotional and Cultural Safety of New Zealand Schools: An Exploration of the Legal Issues. *International Journal of Education Law and Policy (World Conference edition)* 1(1–2): 42–57.

Vialle, W., and J. Paterson. 1996. Fighting for Recognition: Appropriate Educational Approaches to Nurture the Intellectual Potential of Deaf People. Paper presented at the National Deafness Conference, Hobart, Tasmania, Australia, May 22–26.

Victorian School for Deaf Children. 1993. Languages Other Than English (LOTE) Policy [unpublished policy]. Melbourne: Victorian School for Deaf Children.

Waitere-Ang, H., and P. Johnston. 1999. If All Inclusion in Research Means Is the Addition of Researchers That Look Different, Have You Really

Included Me at All? Paper presented at the 1999 AARE-NZARE Conference, Global Issues and Local Effects: The Challenge for Educational Research, Melbourne

Walker, L. M. 1995. An Evaluation of the Reading Comprehension of Students in Victoria Who Are Profoundly, Prelingually Deaf and of an Intervention Program to Improve Their Inferential Reading Comprehension Skills. PhD diss., University of Melbourne, Melbourne.

Walker, L. M. and F. W. Rickards. 1992. Reading Comprehension Levels of Profoundly, Prelingually Deaf Students in Victoria. *The Australian Teacher of the Deaf*, 32, 32–47.

World Federation of the Deaf. 1993. *World Federation of the Deaf Report on the Status of Sign Language*. Finland: Author.

Young, I. M. 1992. Five Faces of Oppression. In *Rethinking Power*, ed. T. E. Wartenberg, 174–95. Albany: State University of New York Press.

Index